GODDESSES & ANGELS

GODDESSES & ANGELS

Awakening Your Inner
High-Priestess and "Source-eress"

Doreen Virtue, PhD

HAY HOUSE
Australia • Canada • Hong Kong
South Africa • United Kingdom • United States

First published and distributed in the United Kingdom by Hay House UK Ltd, Unit 62, Canalot Studios, 222 Kensal Rd, London W10 5BN. Tel.: (44) 20 8962 1230; Fax: (44) 20 8962 1239. www.hayhouse.co.uk

Published and distributed in the United States of America by Hay House, Inc., PO Box 5100, Carlsbad, CA 92018-5100. Tel.: (1) 760 431 7695 or (800) 654 5126; Fax (1) 760 431 6948 or (800) 650 5115. www.hayhouse.com

Published and distributed in Australia by Hay House Australia Ltd, 18/36 Ralph St., Alexandra NSW 2015. Tel.: (61) 2 9669 4299; Fax: (61) 2 9669 4144. www.hayhouse.com.au

Published and distributed in the Republic of South Africa by Hay House SA (Pty), Ltd, PO Box 990, Witkoppen 2068. Tel./Fax: (27) 11 706 6612. orders@psdprom.co.za

Distributed in Canada by Raincoast, 9050 Shaughnessy St., Vancouver, BC V6P 6E5. Tel.: (1) 604 323 7100; Fax: (1) 604 323 2600

Editorial supervision: Jill Kramer • *Design:* Amy Gingery
Interior photos: Steven Farmer • *Underwater photo on page 199*: Dave Ferruolo

A catalogue record for this book is available from the British Library.

ISBN 1-4019-0473-4

Printed and bound in Great Britain by TJ International Ltd, Padstow, Cornwall.

To the Divine feminine spirit, power,
and love that resides within us all.
A bouquet of gratitude to everyone
who helped make this book possible.
Love and blessings to each and
every one of you!

CONTENTS

Introduction

The Sands of Time

I'm riding across the Egyptian desert, escaping persecutors who believe that my teacher's work is dangerous and blasphemous. We're a group of his students, and we've already traveled from Greece to Egypt. We thought Egypt would be our long-term home, but the authorities had other ideas.

I am Ruma, once a young and beautiful woman who caught my teacher's eye. He flirted shamelessly with me until I agreed to study under him. How excited I had been to run away from home and study the secrets of the universe with this man known as Pythagoras. But my excitement soon turned to boredom, as his endless philosophizing seemed pointless to me, and my attention often wandered. I definitely wasn't his best pupil.

Other students came into our fold. The female students were always young and beautiful. As we females aged, Pythagoras gave us less attention. Mature women became support staff—preparing food, straightening sleeping quarters, and making our living space attractive. Attending class was secondary for women, especially as our beauty waned with age, and we garnered less of Teacher's attention.

Now, we're fleeing across the desert. The direction of our travel is secondary to escaping certain death. The wind spits fine white sand across my skin, and I squint to avoid the painful blasts. My hood whips in the wind, spanking my face with each gust. I can't see anyway, as the wind blankets us in a sandy tornado.

I fall onto the sand. My hands are useless in sheltering me from the airborne particles, which seem so tiny and lightweight yet suddenly cover me with their lung-crushing weight. I breathe in and choke. I spit the sand out, but more enters my gaping mouth. Smothered with it, I fight uselessly. I see white everywhere, then gray. Then black.

I float above my body. Small sand dunes cover my friends, our animals, and me. We'd survived the desert heat and the persecutors' weapons, but had succumbed to the fury of the elements. Exactly as Pythagoras had lectured about the mathematical nature of the universe, the sheer number of sand grains had been our undoing.

※ ▨ ※

As I woke up slowly from this past-life regression, I blinked at the sight of white sand surrounding me. But this was no Egyptian desert—my husband, Steven, and I were on a small island in the Australian Great Barrier Reef. We'd rented a motorboat and had brought a picnic to a secluded beach on an uninhabited island. After lunch, Steven had offered to give me a past-life regression to help me overcome my fear of scuba diving.

I'd taken scuba courses for ten years and always panicked during the underwater training in which we had to remove our air supply. These "pretend emergencies" were necessary to learn how to deal with a real one, should the situation arise. Yet the thought of being without air underwater terrified me. I always quit the course at that point.

This wouldn't be a problem, except that I truly wanted to scuba dive. I felt an affinity for the underwater world of fish, coral, and reefs, and I snorkeled at every opportunity. Yet I longed to be a true part of that world, swimming free.

Now at the Great Barrier Reef, I had the chance to dive into the clear turquoise water and see the brightly colored sea landscape and its inhabitants. A German scuba instructor offered to give me a refresher course, which would lead to a Resort Certification so that I could dive.

I had to overcome my fears, so Steven—a skilled metaphysician, shaman, and psychotherapist—had regressed me to the point where the fear had manifested.

Past-life regressions help us release phobias through the process of catharsis, which means letting go of built-up painful emotions.

※ ▨ ※

With my scuba instructor, I begin my first open-water dive at the Great Barrier Reef, Australia.

The surface of the water looks very far away when you're swimming 40 feet below. However, I was more fascinated than afraid, thanks to my past-life regression, which did indeed free me from ancient memories of not having enough air.

I glided through the perfectly transparent turquoise liquid, beside neon-bright coral and giant clamshells. I swam through clouds of yellow butterfly fish, who didn't even flinch at my presence. Like them, I was a sea creature. A mermaid.

A dazzling light show of sun rays danced through the water onto the pearly white sand below me. In my past life, the sand had choked the life out of me. In this one, it acted like a screen projector, reflecting the light and a streaming movie of mermaids, dolphins, undersea castles, wizards, goddesses, and angels.

As I ascended toward the dive boat, I knew two things for sure: one, fear would never again hold me back; and two, I had once lived in the water. I needed to research and remember my underwater lifetime, and teach others what I'd just seen and experienced. Intuitively, I knew that these memories were keys to reclaiming our magical power.

About This Book

This is another chapter in my story of spiritual discovery and adventure, which began with my book *The Lightworker's Way* and continued with its sequels, *Healing with the Fairies* and *Angel Medicine*. However, it's not necessary to read those books to get what you need out of this one.

This is a two-part work, so if you enjoy reading true spiritual adventure stories, then begin with Part I. However, if you're more interested in reading solely about the goddesses and angels who can help you recover your natural spiritual gifts, then Part II is a stand-alone section that you can read first if you choose.

My prayer is that you experience the peace and joy that comes from living, loving, and working with the goddesses and angels.

— Doreen Virtue

✳ ✳ ✳ ✳ ✳ ✳

PART I

ADVENTURES IN SOURCE-ERY

Chapter 1

Full Moon Over Sedona

My first clue that this would be a strange visit to Sedona, Arizona, was when "Gator," a handlebar-mustached taxi driver, pulled in front of our hotel in a dilapidated red Lincoln Town Car. The car's hood sported a large pair of steer horns, and its eight-track tape player blasted a Willie Nelson song.

Gator drove my friend Lynnette Brown (who's also the co-author of my book *Angel Numbers*) and me to a rental-car company. We were in Sedona for the weekend giving a mediumship course. My husband, Steven Farmer, was also in town, co-leading a men's retreat along with Jade Wah'oo, a shamanic teacher.

Sedona is among the most magical places on Earth. The red-rock skyscrapers give it an unearthly appearance. It's easy to feel ungrounded in Sedona, as if you're in a surrealistic dream. During our visit, there was also a harvest moon, the term given to the full moon closest to the autumn equinox, the date when sunlight and nighttime are equal in length as summer ends and fall begins.

I'd become sensitive to the moon's cycles and their effects on my body, moods, and the events I experienced. Full moons elicited adventures and surprises.

I was scheduled to give a speech at the Sedona Creative Life Center on the first evening of our trip. The speech was for WE International, a support group for walk-ins. As I've written in my book *Earth Angels,* walk-ins are spiritually evolved souls who offer to take over the body and life of a depressed or suicidal person, leaving that individual free to go home to Heaven.

Unlike possession, a walk-in situation only involves one soul inhabiting the body. The original soul leaves, and the new walk-in soul enters. The exchange is often done unconsciously, and the only clues that it's happened are when family and friends begin saying, "You've changed so much!" (either as a complaint or a compliment). Walk-in souls usually can't remember their childhood, and they often make sudden changes so their new body's life fits their own personality. It's common for walk-ins to change their first name and leave their spouse, home, and job—all within a short period of time.

As Lynnette and I drove to the venue where I'd be speaking, we called upon Archangel Chamuel to help us find our way. Chamuel is known as the "Finding Angel," as he helps retrieve lost articles and give directions to those who have lost their way.

"Archangel Chamuel, please find the place!" I exclaimed. Then I corrected myself: "I mean, please help *us* find the place!" Lynnette and I chuckled. Otherwise, Chamuel would be at the Sedona Creative Life Center waiting for us, saying, "Well, you asked me to find the place. I've been waiting for you!"

As we laughed, I saw Archangel Michael standing on the side of the road. Michael is a huge, handsome archangel who protects us, and I often invoke him while driving (especially on unfamiliar roads). Michael's bright royal-purple aura lit up the street just as we saw the street sign for Schnebly Hill Road. We turned right on Schnebly and immediately found the center. Thank you, Michael and Chamuel!

Musician Peter Sterling played his harp during the guided meditations, and afterward, he offered to take Lynnette and me to a full-moon ceremony on Cathedral Rock, a monolithic red-rock natural structure that's 900 feet high, almost the same height as Paris's Eiffel Tower.

In addition to its many natural red-rock skyscrapers, Sedona is known for its vortexes, which are energy centers within the earth similar to chakras. Vortexes look like water going down the drain, swirling powerfully in the center. Sensitive people can feel the vortex energy, and many report healings and inspiration from being near them.

"Sedona has four main vortex areas," explained Peter, who had lived in Sedona for many years. He learned to play the harp while listening to the sounds of the Sedona canyons, as well as its angels and fairies. "They are Airport Mesa, Boynton Canyon, Bell Rock, and Cathedral Rock. The vortexes at Airport Mesa and Bell Rock have electrical energy within them. Boynton Canyon's vortex is a combination of electric and magnetic frequencies, while Cathedral Rock's is the only one to be purely magnetic. Since magnetic energy is feminine, Cathedral Rock is a wonderful vortex for women to experience. Its feminine earth energy is very supportive of women and the female body."

The bluish moon lit our pathway as we climbed Cathedral Rock. A group of people with drums and didgeridoos celebrated the full moon at the very top of the rock. Lynnette and I looked at each other, puzzled. *How did they get up there?* we wondered. And I knew that my friend was also thinking the same thing I was: *There's no way I'm going up there!* Peter decided to keep climbing, but Lynnette and I were content at the halfway point.

We selected a flat plateau that was easily accessible. Sitting on the dusty firm ground, I contemplated the panorama around me. I saw crackling sparks of yellow light below the earth's surface, and then I gasped as they formed a female figure that slowly ascended above the ground and appeared before us. It was Artemis, the Grecian moon goddess! Lynnette and I saw her simultaneously.

The Triple Goddess Within

Many people believe that Artemis and the Roman goddess Diana are the same being, but I don't. They look and act completely different: Artemis has a short-cropped pixie haircut, and Diana has tumbling, raven-black locks. Artemis is shy like a forest fairy, while Diana is a bold leader. Their differences continue, but you get my point.

"Go within, go within," Artemis repeated. *"Breathe."* Lynnette and I obediently closed our eyes and breathed deeply to become centered.

Sedona and Lynnette disappeared, and I stood alone on the mountainside with Artemis. She put her hand firmly on my heart, just as the clouds parted and the full moon illuminated her face.

She whispered forcefully, *"Indecision and unclear direction are the heart of the matter. Take small steps toward a unified direction and platform of peace and harmony. Hold steady to this intention and do not waver.*

"Feel the passion of Mother Earth," the goddess went on. *"She continuously gives you embracing, motherly love energy. She embraces you from below, around, and above. Drink in the moonlight on this vortex and replenish your body."*

I began to sway with my deep rhythmic breath as the landscape swirled around me. I feared falling from the high mountain cliff, but Artemis steadied me and repeated: *"Go within. Breathe."* I was afraid that my breath would transport me to an unknown level of existence, an ecstasy I wasn't sure I could handle. I'd just returned from a month's journey through Australia two days earlier—perhaps jet lag was overtaking me. The surreal, dreamlike feelings nearly overwhelmed me, when Artemis spoke again in a soothing voice:

"Breathe in the moonlight and be healed," she cooed. *"Moonlight, like earthly energy, is replenishing and nourishing."* Then she stroked the top of my head. *"Come back into your body, Doreen. You tend to leave and hover above your body during intense experiences. Part of life is learning how to experience all the degrees of feelings."*

I exhaled in the direction of the enormous moon, with full faith that I could release my fatigue and jet lag through my breath with the moon's assistance. A vision danced across the moon's surface, and I saw myself helping the Indigo and Crystal Children, the new psychic and sensitive young people who are often tragically misdiagnosed as being autistic and having attention deficit disorder (ADD). At my talk that evening, I'd spoken about the large number of psychic children who have been prescribed Ritalin in adults' misguided attempt to make them conform. These children don't need drugs; they need our support and guidance in channeling their anger toward positive activism.

I realized that goddess energy means embracing the three parts of the goddess that are naturally within each woman and man, girl and boy: the Maiden (our inner child, who longs to play and express itself); the Mother (that part of us desiring to heal and nurture others); and the Matriarch (representing our desire to teach, and learning to honor our own authority and wisdom). I was being called upon to act from my Matriarch part and teach about the children.

An angel surrounded by a rainbow aura, drawn by a four-year-old Australian girl.

The clouds' moisture reflected around the moon's glow, casting a circular rainbow appearance. I gasped at this sight, realizing that this meant I was also supposed to help the Rainbow Children.

I thought of Karlene MacDonald, a kindergarten teacher for 16 years in the Melbourne, Australia, public schools. During my last visit Down Under, Karlene handed me a painting of an angel made by a four-year-old student. The angel was surrounded by rainbows.

The student had told Karlene, "If the children walked into the rainbows around the angel's head, they would feel very happy!" Then Karlene mentioned that her students' paintings used to contain sunshine and flowers. "But about two years ago, all of my new students began painting rainbows without anyone asking them to."

Although I hadn't yet met any Rainbow Children that I was aware of, the angels had told me that they were the purest souls to yet inhabit our planet. They're the generation that came after the Crystal Children.

Artemis helped me sit down. I removed my sweatshirt and laid my head upon it so that I could fully recline and bathe in the moonlight. I thought of all that I wanted to release to the moon.

There was my fear of speaking up about political matters. On the one hand, I clearly saw and received messages about the world's political landscape. But every time I spoke on these matters, I received complaint letters from folks who insisted I should stick to talking about angels, goddesses, and the like. Yet how could I live with myself if I didn't speak up?!

I thought of the Indigo Children who can't and won't dissociate their feelings. They'll speak up while the rest of us are afraid to. I vowed to nurture the Indigo Children's activism and to help them channel their angst and anger in constructive ways.

Silently I said to myself, *I now release fear. I now release indecision. I now release all pain and suffering I may have absorbed. I now release all drains upon my energy. I now release any blocks to my perfect energy circuit.*

Artemis covered me with a sparkling blanket of moon and star energy, and I slept as if sinking deep into the red Sedona earth. Lynnette's and Peter's voices brought me back to present awareness, and as we walked back to the car, I felt wonderful. My body buzzed with the pleasant energy of being deeply loved. The nurturing that Artemis spoke of felt blissful, and I felt safe in the knowledge that everything was and would be fine with our world.

I realized that when we touch the feminine energy of Mother Earth, we respect her more. A cycle of nurturing then emerges, where we allow Earth to nurture us, and in appreciation, we give back to her. It means getting outside of our homes and offices, turning off the television, and appreciating nature. This is where the Crystal Children help us. Since they love being outdoors all the time, they get their parents to go out, too!

No Logical Override!

The next evening, Steven, Lynnette, and I went to dinner at our hotel's restaurant. Vegetarian selections were sparse on the menu, so we ordered plain salad. I decided to go to our hotel room to retrieve some avocados we'd brought along. Before leaving, a gut feeling told me to take Steven's room key (as well as the one I already had), but I overrode this feeling, deciding it was illogical.

Sure enough, my own room key didn't work, and I had to go back downstairs to get Steven's. Why do we talk ourselves out of these messages? It's like pushing away gifts that are being freely handed to us.

Lynnette, Steven, and I made a pact with ourselves and each other: no logical override of intuition! No matter how illogical the intuitive feelings were, we'd listen to them.

The next morning this pact was put to good use. Lynnette heard an inner voice telling her to get to our workshop room by 8:30 A.M. even though our class wouldn't begin until 10. As she neared the classroom, she understood why she'd been called down so early. Jackhammers pounding outside the door would have totally disrupted the peaceful nature of our mediumship workshop! Since Lynnette had gotten there so early, she had plenty of time to negotiate with the workers and hotel staff to stop the hammering before we began.

We kept our mediumship courses small, with no more than 28 students, so I could hear and see each person's readings. That allowed Lynnette and me to personally guide each person through any blocks or challenges. We'd learned from previous classes that if we just patiently worked with each student, everyone could give a mediumship reading by the third day of class.

One student in our Sedona mediumship course named Gary Wiler was already a professional medium. Gary's readings were detailed, accurate, and compassionate, but he'd come to the course to gain confidence in his ability to give readings at public workshops.

On the last day of the class, Lynnette and I performed a psychic ceremony on the students, using crystals, tuning forks, and essential oils. First, I held a giant clear quartz crystal up to each person's brow and used visualization and intention to send a burst of white light through the crystal. I also placed my left hand's index finger on the back of each person's head to send additional white light. This allowed the third eye's optic nerve to be cleaned, much like clearing a clogged drain.

As I sent light to my students, I psychically looked at their third eye for any debris that could block their spiritual sight. I then increased the width of their third eye's optic nerve to increase the clarity of their psychic visions.

Each person's third eye looked different to me. For instance, I noticed that Gary's third eye was extremely bloodshot, as if it had been crying. I sent him extra white light, like a form of energetic eyedrops. His third eye gratefully accepted the gift, and the redness left.

People who are afraid of seeing angels or spirit guides often have debris covering their third eye, which looks like bugs splattered on a windshield. White light easily clears this away, provided that the person is open to seeing the spirit world. I have to assure those who are fearful of experiencing clairvoyance that the angels and spirit guides are among the most beautiful sights in the world. To me, seeing angels is akin to swimming with gorgeous tropical fish (probably since that's my idea of great beauty). I assure my students that the grotesque images of the afterlife in movies aren't accurate. If they've been able to sit through a scary movie, they've seen things ten times worse than they'll ever see in the spirit world.

Seeing spirits and angels is a choice, just like deciding to ski down a mountain slope or travel to an exotic location. It's among the most exciting of experiences, and it can take your life to new heights.

❉ ❉ ❉ ❉ ❉ ❉

Chapter 2

THE GODDESS IN THE SWEAT LODGE

As Steven and I pulled into the driveway, the carved wooden thunderbird atop Jade Wah'oo's Sedona home told me that we were in for quite an experience. Jade was conducting a sweat-lodge ceremony following the men's retreat that he and Steven led.

Sweat lodges are Native American–based ceremonies held within the confines of a small building or tent. Hot rocks smolder in the enclosure, and everyone sits in the dark, sweating away physical and spiritual impurities. Most people have visions and insights during these ceremonies, so I was excited and a bit nervous, as I'd never attended one before.

The magical energy of the Sedona desert made the sweat lodge that much more inviting. The weekend mediumship workshop that Lynnette and I had given had been intense. Lynnette caught an early-morning flight back to her home in Laguna Beach, while Steven and I decided to stay in Sedona for another day to attend Jade's sweat lodge. Having known Jade for several years, Steven and I trusted him to lead us through a safe and meaningful ceremony.

Besides Steven, Jade, and me, we were joined by old friends Bruce and Vicky Bellman, and Jade's neighbors Joan and Paivi.

As Jade instructed, we drank lots of water beforehand and had one last toilet break before beginning the ceremony. Dressed in swimsuits and shorts, we all stood in a circle around an open fire pit filled with hot stones. Jade threw the herb sweetgrass into the fire to purify its energy.

"What would you like to dedicate this sweat lodge to?" Jade asked Steven and me.

"Gratitude," answered Steven.

"The power of the goddess," I answered.

I wondered whether the dark enclosure would make me claustrophobic. I'd heard stories of people dashing anxiously out of sweat lodges, and wondered whether I'd do the same.

Just then, two petite quail birds walked nearby. Their peaceful cooing calmed me.

Jade's son acted the part of "Raven," the traditional title of the fire-tender who stays outside during these ceremonies. Dressed all in black, he certainly looked like a raven. He would bring hot rocks, water, and various items (a feather to wave the smoke, sweetgrass to purify the air and energy, and a rattle to call upon Spirit) into our enclosure during the ceremony.

The sweat lodge was a tent covered with 28 crossbars made of bowed willow-sapling wood, representing the ribs of a bear. One horizontal bar represented the bear's spine. At the front of the tent, an altar held a bear skull. As we walked inside, I felt as if I were entering a mother bear's womb.

Our ceremony was scheduled for four rounds, meaning that Raven would bring in seven new hot stones four times. Part spiritual journey and part endurance test, I wondered if I'd make it through the entire ritual.

Inside the tent, we selected places to sit around the pit of hot stones. I sat as far away from the heat as possible, settling in cross-legged upon towels to absorb perspiration. Jade pointed to the largest stone in the pit. "This is the heart of the bear!" he said authoritatively. Then he called for the tent flap to be closed. We were enveloped in utter darkness.

As my eyes adjusted, I noticed a dot of light from the corner of the tent near me. *Oh good!* I thought. *That means air is coming through as well as light.*

Unfortunately, Jade saw the light, too. "Raven, my son," he said, "there's a streak of light. Please close it up!" With that command, the tent became black and hot.

Jade lit sandalwood, and the group began chanting, "So-she-ket-zel," which I gathered was the name of a being I didn't recognize and couldn't pronounce. Unsure of their invocation and wanting to conserve energy, I sat back silently. Jade continued chanting as he ladled water over the rocks. Steam hissed and filled the tent. We each said a prayer, one by one. With each prayer, Jade poured water on the rocks. Soon, the tent was so hot and steamy that sweat poured from my face and body, and my small towel was saturated.

My heart pounded and raced, my body reacting as if I were in trouble. How was my physiology to know I'd entered this process purposefully and I wasn't in danger? Or was I? Perhaps my body knew more than my well-meaning mind. I thought of the students from my mediumship class who had complained of physical ailments stemming from performance anxiety. I remembered how I'd endured similar fears during my first attempts at scuba diving.

I laid down on another towel and felt cool air from the corner of the tent that had shed light. I put my mouth near the tiny hole and gasped futilely to inhale the outside air. My heart continued to pound, and I feared having an anxiety attack that would force me to abandon the ceremony. I prayed for assistance to help me endure, and even enjoy, the experience.

I blinked in the dark as a glowing figure stood before me. The tent was too short for anyone to stand upright, yet a woman was standing and looking at me. She was clearly Native American, with long silky black hair, a youthful 30-something-looking face, and a white animal-skin dress with fringe and red beads. She was beautiful, loving, and compassionate.

The woman wordlessly conveyed to me that everything was going to be okay. Her message reassured me, but it was her angelic energy that calmed me with its enveloping love. Then I realized that this was the being whom Jade and the group had invoked at the beginning of the ceremony! He'd asked this being—whose name sounded like "So-she-ket-zel"—to watch over us. And she was doing that with me.

I calmed down just as the first round of the ceremony ended, meaning that Jade momentarily lifted the tent flap. The outside desert air was 89 degrees, yet it was much cooler than our tent's hot and steamy atmosphere. Raven passed a ladle of water into the tent. Each person sipped from it and passed it clockwise to the next person. By the time the ladle reached me, it was nearly empty.

"Please, sir, may I have some more?" I said in an Oliver Twist accent, and began passing the ladle back to Raven. Hands blocked the ladle as Jade explained, "When the ladle's empty, it's never passed over the stones or clockwise. It's passed back around the circle of the group, counterclockwise."

So many rules! I thought, passing the ladle to my right. When the refilled ladle reached me, I gratefully drank, not caring that others had sipped from the same container. It was the best-tasting water I'd ever had.

After our brief respite, Jade announced the second round by lighting sweetgrass. "This makes for a sweet and pleasant residing place for Spirit," he explained as Raven shoveled in seven more red-hot stones. Down went the tent flap, along with the light and fresh air. I heard the hiss of steam as Jade ladled water into the pit.

I felt my fears rise again, but then remembered the beautiful woman. Although I couldn't see her, I now felt her calming presence beside me, like a wise friend who knew there was nothing to be afraid of. I'd come so far with overcoming fears, and the sweat lodge would be my personal victory over anxiety.

The dread I'd felt about scuba diving had been uprooted as a result of my past-life regression to my Egyptian past. That one regression had freed me of a gripping fear that had previously appeared in other ways.

There was the time, for instance, when Steven wanted to commemorate my decision to work without a manager and alter my workshop travel schedule for the better. As the author of the book *Sacred Ceremony,* Steven frequently conducts ceremonies to mark, heal, or celebrate our life passages. For this ceremony, Steven took me to the beach with several friends.

"We're going to bury your old way of working," Steven explained as he directed everyone to dig a grave-like ditch in the sand. When the ditch was two feet deep, Steven asked me to lie down. He covered my face and body with two beach blankets and put a large straw in my mouth "to breathe air when you're buried with sand," he said as I gulped. "You'll also have one hand above the sand, and if there's any problem with the weight of the sand, just move your hand around and we'll dig you up immediately."

The ceremony sounded tame enough, and it definitely symbolized releasing my old way of working. As they shoveled sand on top of me, I called upon Archangel Michael to protect me. My breathing slowed as the surprisingly heavy sand piled upon my chest and lungs.

The sand kept coming, and I felt completely blanketed as I breathed through the straw. I tried to shift my body but found I couldn't move. That's when panic set in. I moved my hand to signal Steven and my friends to uncover me, but no one noticed. I snapped my fingers, and I heard my friend Becky Prelitz say, "I think she's trying to tell us something." I made a "Stop!" motion with my extended hand and fingers.

"Do you want us to stop?" Steven asked.

How could I signal *Yes*, I wondered? I motioned my thumb upward to signal my desire to come up for air.

"Does that mean that everything's okay?" he asked.

No! I screamed in my mind. *Get me out of here, now! I'm buried alive, and if you don't get me out of here, you'll find a corpse who died of fear!*

My various hand movements finally conveyed my panic to everyone, and they dug me out quickly. Shaking the sand off of me, I sat down to contemplate what had set off my intense anxiety. I'd had a similar episode during a spa treatment in which my arms and hands were wrapped next to my body like a mummy. I'd lasted about three minutes before uncoiling my arms from the tincture-slathered wrapping.

Now I understand that the sandstorm in Egypt was the culprit. Since I'd been able to heal that fear, I should be able to withstand the fear that this sweat lodge is bringing up, I thought. *I need to face and move through my insecurities.*

Jade's booming voice jolted me out of introspection, and I realized that Round 2 had ended. Hey! I was surviving this after all! We were halfway through, and my energy was still holding up.

After we sipped more water from the ladle, Jade announced that the third round would be the most intense in duration and heat. "Bring me the hottest stones you have!" Jade called to Raven, who shoveled huge red glowing rocks into the tent's pit. Jade placed copal resin on the stones. Copal is also known as "the tears of the tree of life"—sap that Mesoamericans consider to be Mother Earth's tears. It's used to purify and protect during ceremonies.

Jade explained that the third round's intensity would help everyone surrender their defenses so that they could bridge their own soul. The heat would draw out old pain and wounds so healing could begin.

I wasn't prepared for the hot wall of air radiating against my head. I'd perspired all I could in the previous two rounds, so I lay my dehydrated body down and slid my mouth to the tiny hole in the tent's corner. Sucking on whatever scraps of air I could find, I drew them in rhythmically.

I thought that Steven was petting me, but then I realized that the beautiful Native American woman had returned to my side. As she gently cooed like a dove, her breath cooled me. She then embraced me, and I embraced her back. When the round was over, I felt elated that I'd endured the experience.

As the fourth round began, I felt like I was at the tail end of a marathon. I was nearly done, and would hang on until the end.

Jade placed bear root on the fresh supply of hot stones. He explained that this herb was local to the Rocky Mountains and was used as an all-purpose tincture to represent the body of the Earth Mother. "The theme of Round 4 is appreciation and integration," Jade announced as the tent flapped shut. When the ceremony was over, we took turns spraying each other with Jade's garden hose. Giddy with exhaustion and delight, we played in the water like little kids.

After we'd all showered and changed into comfortable clothing, we gathered in Jade's house, with its amazing views of the Sedona peaks. As we shared a potluck buffet of healthful foods, I felt extra relaxed. Having shared this experience with the people around me, I felt comfortable with them all.

I took Jade aside and described the woman I'd seen. "Why, that's Xochiquetzal!" he exclaimed. "Don't you remember? We invoked her during the first round of the ceremony!" I asked him to spell the name for me, as I hadn't heard it before. He pronounced her name for me slowly as "Zo-she-ket-zel," and I repeated it until I'd memorized the name.

"She's like an angel," I said. "Who is she?"

I learned that Xochiquetzal is an Aztec and Toltec goddess also known as "Flower Feather." She's an earth- and fire-element fertility goddess who inspires love and passion. She's also considered a protective Mother goddess, which she certainly had been for me during the sweat-lodge ceremony.

As we were leaving Jade's house to drive back to Laguna Beach, Steven handed me a fragrant flower. This seemed extra fitting, considering that Xochiquetzal is a flower goddess. As I enjoyed the flower's aroma, I continued to feel Xochiquetzal's loving protection for the entire drive home.

※ ※ ※ ※ ※ ※

Chapter 3

HEALING WITH THE
HARMONIC CONCORDANCE

Back home in Laguna Beach, Lynnette and I were teaching another mediumship course. I received countless requests to present this course throughout the world, but after conducting it in Miami and Sedona, I'd learned that the workshop required so much of my energy that I needed to teach it from my home base. There was something about sleeping in my own bed at night that kept my energy at the high level required.

I taught the students the same lessons the spirit world had taught me when I was first conducting mediumship sessions. The spirit world had been my firm but patient teacher, often chastising me for doing things like "hit-and-run readings" (where I'd contact a deceased person, ask them for a message, and then get distracted before he or she could respond).

"There are three parts to giving a mediumship reading," I told the students. "First, you need to define how the deceased person you're talking to is related to your client. Are you receiving messages from the client's grandparent, parent, sibling, friend, spouse, or child? You can determine the relationship by discerning where the deceased person is standing next to your client.

"Ask your client which hand they write with. If they're a right-handed person, then the right side of their body is their 'male' side, and the left side of their body is their 'female' side. The opposite is true in a person born left-handed (even if they were forced to become right-handed while growing up).

"Paternal relatives will appear behind your client's male side, and the maternal relatives are behind their left side. The closer the deceased person stands to your client's head, the closer their genealogical relationship. So, departed parents stand behind the client's head. Grandparents appear above the client's shoulders, and more distant relatives appear to the client's side. Friends, siblings, children, and lovers are on the client's female side."

Then I taught the students the second part of a mediumship reading, which is to give the client at least one specific detail about their deceased loved one.

"There's an old Irish saying: 'If you meet a leprechaun on the road, he won't tell you his name.' That's because if you knew his name, you'd know everything about him. Everyone's first name carries a unique energy fingerprint, even if you have a common name. Like a snowflake, no two first names carry the same energy.

"When someone says your first name, they can feel your essence. That's why the most important 'marketing tool' is to keep your energy clean through processes such as meditation and integrity. People will be attracted to your first name if you keep your energy clean and high.

"You can get information about any person or animal, living or deceased, by saying their first name repeatedly. If they've changed their first name, try the new version and see if it gives you information and impressions. If not, use the birth name."

The class practiced this on a few people in the class who said the names of their deceased loved ones. Everyone was able to access accurate information through this method. "You can also get information about a city, country, company, movie, or project by saying its name repeatedly," I added.

Then I taught the class the third part of a mediumship session: the message of love. "Even though you as a medium may feel embarrassed or bored by delivering sentimental messages, this is the most healing part of the session," I reminded the students. "The deceased will apologize, give etheric roses, and send loving messages through you. Your client needs to hear these messages to heal away guilt, anger, worries, and fear, which are all a part of grief."

preservatives to others. For instance, alcohol (including organically produced wine and beer) contains naturally occurring sulfites, and more are added during distillation. Vinegar and pickled products all have sulfites, and many dried fruit and canned goods are preserved with them. Tofu is sometimes preserved with sulfur-containing chemicals, and salad bars are frequently sprayed with sulfites to prevent lettuce-browning.

So, my usual diet of a salad topped with vinaigrette dressing and sulfite-preserved tofu with a glass of wine was making my body bloat and itch.

Thank you, angels, for helping me discover the cause of my discomfort!

Shifting the Inner Goddess

Taking Michael's guidance to detoxify my body, drink green powder with juice daily, and abstain from sulfites, I lost 45 pounds rapidly. I felt lighter and more energized, but even more, I noticed a shift in my triple-goddess archetype. As I mentioned earlier, within each woman and man exists the three aspects of the goddess: the playful, sexy, and innocent Maiden; the nurturing and giving Mother; and the Matriarch, who teaches and shares her wisdom. (I prefer the term *Matriarch* to the term *Crone,* which is traditionally used in goddess studies.)

As I detoxified, I became aware of how I'd approached many of my relationships as a Mother. I was always the one who gave time, nurturing, money, and other aspects of caring. Sometimes I resented the disproportionate amounts I gave, without feeling that anything was returning to me.

In my lighter body, I not only looked less matronly, but I also felt like the slimmer and trimmer Maiden and Matriarch aspects of the goddess. I no longer wanted any unbalanced relationship in which I was the sole giver.

I began avoiding a girlfriend named Andrea (not her real name) with whom I'd had an unbalanced Mother-Daughter relationship. We'd both shared a lot when we were single, but after I'd married, I tired of listening to her continual struggles in the dating world. At the beginning of our relationship, I'd made the mistake of giving and spices on my salads. Alcohol was gone, along with the pickled artichoke hearts and olives I'd frequently eaten. My weight melted off effortlessly with these subtle changes.

In addition to my road-weariness, I was on the tail end of healing from a chemical face peel I'd had one week earlier. This was my third such peel, and probably my last, I'd decided. Sure, they were a fast way to erase facial wrinkles, but at what cost? They were so painful, and after the procedure, I felt as disfigured as the Phantom of the Opera, while my skin dried crispy brown and peeled away. For four days, I hid at home so no one except close friends and family could see me.

(Why do we women endure painful procedures in the name of beauty? Is there that much pressure to stay a perpetual Maiden? Why can't we embrace the aging Matriarch as a beautiful aspect of goddesshood? Why are women counseled to cut their hair short, wear long sleeves, high-necked shirts, and loose clothing as soon as any signs of aging occur? Can't we embrace aging hair and skin as a sign of beauty, instead of masking it?)

Steven's appointment in the crystal bed was first, so I dropped him off and drove to the Mother's Market health-food store on 17th Street in Costa Mesa.

I heard my name called at the store and turned around to see Andrea, the girlfriend I'd been avoiding. She looked horrified upon seeing my peeling face and asked, "Have you been in an accident?" I explained I'd had a facial peel, and she relaxed and smiled.

"Where have you been?" she asked.

I squirmed to come up with an answer. How could I blurt out, "I've been avoiding you!" there in the produce section of the grocery store? So I said, "Well, I've been traveling." (Which was true, I reassured myself.)

Then, as we'd done so many times before, the energy shifted as soon as I asked Andrea how she was. Andrea began telling me about her financial troubles, her career crisis, and how her latest boyfriend had betrayed her. My body tightened at the familiarity of the scenario, and I noticed that I was backing away. Although I genuinely cared about Andrea, as I listened to her diatribe I realized that she expected, and therefore continually created, drama for herself. *I'll tell her someday,* I vowed to myself. *But not today.*

"I've got to go!" (Which was the truth, since my crystal-bed appointment time was nearing.) Then I hugged Andrea and left the store.

The Healing Chamber

I walked into the lobby and met Chris Marmes, a girlfriend and local psychic healer who is soft-spoken and has the gentle energy that comes from years of devoted meditating. She was keenly interested in Kelly's crystal-healing bed and his methods, and she'd come to study both. *What a contrast to Andrea,* I thought, as Chris stared into my eyes with great presence and asked how I was. *She really cares!* I realized. *This is the energy of true friendship.*

"Would you like to be with me in my healing session?" I asked her.

Chris doesn't talk much, but her expression conveyed her answer: "Yes, if you're okay with my being there."

Since I trusted Chris and didn't yet know Kelly except through friends' recommendations, I motioned for her to come with me. Steven lay on a massage table with a metal frame hanging overhead. Seven enormous crystal points hung from the frame, each crystal pointing toward one of his seven major chakras. Colored lights corresponding to each chakra color (red for the base chakra, and so on) flashed behind each crystal. A machine controlling the speed of the flashing lights whirred in the background.

The machine and flashing lights slowed, and Steven opened his eyes. We looked at each other and smiled. His blue eyes radiated deep relaxation and contentment. I didn't need to ask him how he was or how he'd enjoyed his session. His bright eyes and renewed energy said everything.

Steven slowly stood up and helped me onto the massage table. Six clear quartz crystals stared down at me, sparkling like perfect energy conveyers. Pointing at my root chakra was a beige smoky quartz, a crystal known as a "psychic vacuum cleaner" for its ability to clear away emotional toxins.

The energy of the large crystals made me feel spacey, as if I were in a waking dream. I closed my eyes as Kelly entered the room. A former Navy Seal, Kelly was a big macho man with an engineer's mind and a spirit-seeker's heart. Exhausted from all my traveling, I prayed for protection to help me relax into the session.

I saw the Greek warrior goddess, Athena, at my side like a powerful nurse in attendance during surgery. She paced and watched Kelly, and I felt safe enough to close my eyes again and surrender to the healing session.

As soon as I surrendered, I understood the reason for Athena's presence. The flickering lights behind the crystal points took me straight back to past-life memories of the Atlantean healing temples, which also featured therapeutic crystal beds. In Atlantis, the strong Mediterranean sunlight filtered through a hole at the temple's rooftop and was directed to a pyramid altar beneath the hole. The pyramid of light would bounce onto crystal points that we priestesses held above our patients' chakras on polished concave beds carved of solid crystal.

As in the Atlantis temples, Kelly's healing work involved pulling energetic toxins from his patient's aura. First, I saw him pull a big black spidery mass from my throat chakra. I had a vision of a person jealous of my speaking career throwing a curse my way that had manifested as this spider. A neophyte would have thrown the curse right back at her, but I knew that such an action would have devastating consequences for myself and the other person. So I chose to pray for her well-being and healing instead. My success comes from using my power—the same power we're all born with—with love. Those who misuse their power experience struggles with life, including blocks in manifesting their goals.

Next, Kelly extracted an elderly husband and wife who attached to me during a mediumship session. They were loving, but I realized that they were one reason for my recent fatigue. As they left, my energy level rose dramatically. I protected myself during mediumship work by invoking Archangel Michael and visualizing white light around myself. Yet, during my intense seminar tours, I sometimes forgot to protect myself at smaller book-signing events. The couple hadn't possessed me in the scary sense; they were simply misguided hitchhikers whom I hadn't noticed due to my tiredness.

The flashing lights through the crystals felt wonderful. No darkness could hide in the bright light of this machine, along with Kelly's pure intentions and the prayers emitted by Chris (who sat nearby during the session).

I felt Kelly's presence near my head. Opening my eyes partway, I saw him yanking a big black bulb out of the top of my head. Like a gardener pulling a stubborn weed, Kelly's biceps bulged as he struggled to extract the entity through my crown chakra. A golden hue of light emanated from Kelly, but it wasn't purely from his own aura. Standing behind him was a team of beautiful and powerful goddesses: I saw Aine, the Celtic fairy queen; Aphrodite, the Greek love goddess; Maeve, the Celtic goddess who explained that she was helping me with perimenopausal issues; and of course, Athena.

A vision of the Atlantean healing temple overtook my awareness. Then it hit me: Although I'd administered countless healings to our patients at the temple, I'd never *received* treatment myself. And I'd continued this same unbalanced pattern of giving without receiving in my present lifetime.

I also saw how many times I'd feigned interest while listening to someone's complaints, and how this energetically lowered me. I needed to be completely *authentic* with others. Integrity demanded that I not be "fake nice" and pretend to be interested in others' negative stories. If I were to truly awaken my inner high-priestess, I needed to courageously speak my truth with love.

I thought of Louise Hay, one of my heroes and mentors and someone whom I've been fortunate enough to travel with while giving workshops. One time Louise and I were eating lunch in Denver when someone approached me for an autograph. Louise said very matter-of-factly: "We're eating lunch right now. You'll need to talk to Doreen afterward." Louise masterfully said what was on her mind, with disarming power and grace. She showed no sign of guilt or remorse for being truthful.

Kelly continued pulling psychic debris out of my body and aura. At the end of the session, he reminded me of Archangel Michael after an arduous clash with dark forces.

Once I'd regained full awareness of my surroundings, I faced my healer. His expression belied his distress, and I thought, *This is why I don't schedule many healings for myself! Just like my long hair exhausts my hairdresser, my world-weary aura challenges healers.*

Kelly spoke slowly and deliberately. "That was the toughest battle I've ever waged. You've *got* to shield yourself better!"

I'd received the same scolding from Dolores Cannon, the hypnotherapist and author of *Conversations with Nostradamus*, when she'd regressed me back to my lifetime as a Babylonian priest-astronomer. During the session, Dolores had hypnotized me into a full trance state and then asked me questions, with a tape recorder capturing everything I said. My unconscious mind spoke to Dolores about my present lifetime, demanding that I psychically shield myself more consistently.

Since I did healing work virtually continuously, including during my dreamtimes, I was often in an altered state—so much so that I hadn't driven a car on freeways since the mid-1990s, since I didn't trust that I was grounded enough to drive fast. With my frequent altered states and busy healing schedule, I often forgot to shield myself.

Shielding involves visualizing a protective film of light around yourself or another person or object. This light acts as a filter, allowing only love to pass through. Any lower energies are transmuted by the light. White light is the living, intelligent essence of angels, so when you visualize white light around an object or a person, you're invoking angels to protect it. The light shield wears off after about 12 hours, so it needs to be reinvoked. In intense and fearful situations, the light wears off even quicker.

On the drive home, Steven said, "Kelly's warrior background as a Navy Seal and former police officer is perfect for his Light Warrior work."

I told Steven about my insights during the crystal-healing session. "Shielding and being authentic is honoring the goddess within me." I asked Athena and Archangel Michael to remind me to shield myself consistently.

❈ ❈ ❈ ❈ ❈ ❈

Chapter 5

Home in Laguna Beach

As we walked out of the Wild Oats Community Market, Steven waved hello to a man in the parking lot.

Laguna Beach is an artists' community filled with many colorful and magical people, and John, the man whom Steven had greeted, was among them. John specialized in painting fairy portraits.

"Meet Dovena!" exclaimed John, as he extended his hand to show us a small brown dove. I was transfixed as the dove's gentle energy and beautiful gaze instantly opened and warmed my heart.

"Would you like to hold her?" John asked, handing her to me. Dovena sat in my hand as John explained how he'd found her as a baby with a broken wing. He'd nursed Dovena back to health, and although she was free to fly away, she chose to stay with John as a pet. Dovena closed her eyes and relaxed in my hand. I felt tremendous surges of loving energy that could only be described as goddess-like. She allowed me to stroke her, and I felt nurtured and healed. Here was a pure-of-heart healer whom I felt safe to receive from.

The Crystal Concert

The next day, Steven and I attended a concert at L.A. Outback, a Laguna Beach store specializing in Australian items such as the didgeridoo, outback clothing, and Aboriginal art. Since Steven and

I took annual trips to Australia, we were especially fond of the store. The owner, Barry, always greeted us with "How're you going?"—a phrase unique to the land Down Under.

Ash Dargan of Darwin, Australia (the northern territory rich with Aboriginal communities), played the didgeridoo with the energetic style of a jazz musician. Then Barry announced that Ash would be accompanied by a new musician named Evren Ozan.

As Evren walked out onto the stage, we all gasped. He was a boy! At age 11, Evren had already recorded two best-selling CDs (in the top 20 on the New Age charts). His long blonde hair, teen-idol good looks, and slight frame were fascinating to watch. Not only that, but Evren's large eyes, peaceful energy, and the way he communicated through music and spoke very little showed that he was a Crystal Child.

Evren first discovered the native flute when he was six years old during a family vacation to the Grand Canyon. His parents stopped at a shop where Evren selected a cedar flute, paid for it with all of his allowance, and began playing without lessons. The next year at age seven, he recorded his first album called *Images of Winter,* followed by a second album called *As Things Could Be,* which Backroads Music awarded one of 2003's best instrumental albums.

The cherubic musician closed his eyes and smiled blissfully as he played for us. His music held much loving energy, and I realized that Evren was healing people through his songs. Like many Crystal Children, he was a natural-born healer. Between songs, Evren simply bowed and said, "Thank you." Another Crystal characteristic is that they communicate nonverbally (and, unfortunately, are often misdiagnosed with autism or Asperger's syndrome because they don't begin speaking until age three or four). Evren obviously communicated through his music.

After the concert, Steven spoke with Ash about playing didgeridoo music on the CD for his forthcoming book, *Power Animals,* which Ash readily agreed to do. I spoke with Evren's mother, Faith, and she agreed that he'd play music at my Angel Therapy Practitioner certification courses.

Full-Moon Healing

On December 8, the moon shone bright and full into the room where I was receiving a massage from Ayurvedic doctor Shannon Kennedy. With her long blonde hair, large eyes, and full lips, Shannon could pass for a model. Yet her thirst for healing wisdom, along with her marriage to Reza, an Ayurvedic astrologer, had spurred her education in Eastern traditions.

In fact, Shannon was so beautiful inside and out that I could have easily felt threatened that such a lovely woman was going to be massaging my husband. However, she's passionately in love with her own spouse, and she also possesses a purity that puts me completely at ease.

Shannon is well read and often relays information to me on subjects that she knows I'm interested in. That evening she told me about a scientific article contending that humankind's physiology more closely resembled a manatee than a chimpanzee. This was additional evidence about our water origins, and I vowed to find out more.

Full moons are a wonderful time to release anything you don't want. So, after the massage, Steven and I sat on reclining chairs on our patio deck to take a moon bath and perform a releasement ceremony.

We first discussed what we wanted to release. I realized that I'd been harboring unrealistic guilt that I wasn't doing enough for my children, parents, and Steven. With these insights, my determination, and the full moon's support, I vowed to release these feelings.

As we sat under the moonlight, a large bright star sparkled red, blue, and pink, like a giant crystal magnifying a spotlight. I asked Steven which star this was.

"That's the Dog Star, Sirius," he replied, explaining that the star was Orion's dog in the constellation.

Various cultures claimed that their goddess came from this star. For instance, the ancient Egyptians considered Sirius the birthplace of their goddesses Sopdet and Isis. In later times, the Egyptians said that Sirius was the embodiment of the dog belonging to Osiris and his sister/wife Isis.

For the full-moon ceremony, Steven placed a metal bucket next to us, and then he lit some sage to clear the area around us. We'd each written what we wanted to release on a piece of paper. We began the ceremony with an invocation, in which I called on all of the goddess energy within and around me to fully emerge and awaken. I said, "As the last full moon of 2003, I ask that all of the old energy and imbalances be released fully."

We then read our papers to each other, set them on fire, and threw them into the bucket together. I felt self-imposed burdens lift from my shoulders as the papers burned under the moonlight. Now the massage Shannon had given me earlier was truly complete.

※ ※ ※ ※ ※ ※

Chapter 6

MAYAN MYSTERY SCHOOL

We'd been invited to Cancún, Mexico, by Ivonne Delaflor, a woman who had read my books about Indigo and Crystal Children. Ivonne is passionate about helping children, and she's the patron of a Mexican orphanage.

Ivonne sent a car to retrieve us from the busy Cancún airport and whisk us to the Ritz-Carlton Hotel, where we were to be her guests. Our suite overlooked the Mexican Riviera's turquoise water, and although it was nearly Christmas, the beach was a summertime tropical scene, with scantily clad bathers and people riding Jet Skis and parasailing.

Ivonne invited us to dinner that evening. As Steven and I waited to meet her in the lavishly decorated lobby, we listened to someone playing and singing a lively rendition of Billy Joel's "Piano Man" in the hotel bar.

As the song finished, a beautifully dressed young woman walked up to us and introduced herself: "Hello, you must be Steven and Doreen. I'm Ivonne Delaflor, which means 'I am of the flowers.'"

"Like the fairies!" I said, without realizing that fairies might not be the best topic to bring up to make a favorable first impression when meeting someone new.

"Yes!" She smiled, and both of us were clearly relieved to meet a person who "believed."

As we walked to the restaurant behind Ivonne, who was busily greeting hotel employees, Steven and I talked. "Whom did Ivonne say she was bringing to meet us at dinner?" he asked me.

"I think she said his name was Alex," I replied.

"And what did she say Alex did? An anthropologist? An archaeologist?"

The memory of what Ivonne had said during our brief first meeting in the lobby had been a blur. She'd said so much of importance, describing the orphan children, her workshops, and her passion for helping others.

Then I remembered. "He's a Mayan astrologer," I said. Steven nodded. My head spun with the implications of meeting with Ivonne and Alex in Cancún. Finally, I could ask knowledgeable experts about the Mayan calendar and numerology. It was going to be an interesting few days, I thought, as my stomach lurched with the same sensation Alice must have felt falling down the rabbit hole. We were going to experience and learn some mind-bending things.

The maître d' escorted us into a posh marble-floored, high-ceilinged, gilded restaurant, where Ivonne introduced us to Alex Sleiki. Alex was a tall young Mexico City resident, Mayan astrologer, angel channeler, and playwright. He shyly admitted that he was the one we'd heard playing and singing "Piano Man" earlier.

As we sat for dinner, attentive waiters doted on us, and Ivonne explained her background. In 1989, on the Mexican Day of the Dead, she was riding in a car that smashed into a concrete wall. Right before the impact, Ivonne saw a vision of Mother Mary on the wall. Ivonne's right arm was detached in the crash, but she didn't bleed at all. She fully credits Mary for saving her life and her arm, which was surgically reattached.

Alex explained that he'd always been sensitive and had even seen spirits in childhood. The spirits helped Alex cope with his intense young life. His father had died when he was 12, and the next year he discovered that his brother was adopted. The year after, his mother remarried, and finances forced the family to move into a cramped apartment. Transcendental Meditation helped Alex heal these emotional wounds, and the following year one of his teachers suggested that Alex try automatic writing. This led to Alex communicating with the angels and the spirit world.

Alex then began explaining Mayan astrology: "The system is based on 13 houses." That made sense, considering that the Mexican culture was matriarchal and honored the mother and feminine energy. The number 13 is revered in cultures that embrace the power of the 13 annual cycles of the moon and women. In cultures that fear the power of the moon and women; however, 13 is considered unlucky.

"Mayan astrology helps us to understand and assess Tzolkin," Alex continued, explaining that this Mayan word (pronounced *SOUL-keen*) means "Do I live what I believe?" Mayan astrology is a system to discover your life's purpose, and Alex explained that each astrological sign has an animal spirit guide. His is a Pegasus (a winged horse) and a serpent.

"In the Mayan tradition, the serpent (which represents the body) and the eagle (which represents the spirit) are very important," he said. "We believe, and our prophecy predicts, that the serpent and the eagle must unite, as they're depicted on the Mexican flag."

I was intrigued, even though I didn't quite understand the full impact of what Alex meant. Yet I trusted that I'd soon learn the hidden meanings during this journey.

Alex pulled out a Mayan astrological reference wheel and asked for my birth date. When I replied, "April 29, 1958," Alex exclaimed, "No wonder!"

I leaned forward to see what he was pointing to. The wheel looked nothing like traditional astrological symbols, so I asked Alex to explain.

"You're a dragon being led by a serpent! In Mayan astrology, the dragon's motto is: 'I nurture the self with the power of being.' The dragon represents the Buddha self. Dragon is a protector of wholeness and the mind. Dragon corresponds to the number 8, which means harmony, integrity, role-modeling, and prosperity. You're a shaman or a wizard, according to Mayan astrology."

That sure sounded good, even if I didn't completely understand it. I wondered where I could find more information on Mayan spirituality. As if she were reading my thoughts, Ivonne handed me a book called *Chichén Itzá*.

Where did this come from? Ivonne hadn't carried anything into the restaurant, yet the book had virtually materialized the moment I'd desired it.

Ivonne explained that she'd thought about giving me a book, when a waiter walked by and handed her *that* book, which she then gave to me.

Whoa! I shuddered. I hadn't seen any waiter with a book. Clearly, Ivonne was a Divine alchemist who could instantly manifest desires into reality. Yet it was my desire that had set the manifestation into motion. *Trippy stuff!*

The waiters brought our food on fine china. The chef had kindly made me a sulfite-free dish with tofu and fresh Mexican papaya. The candlelight and chandeliers, live piano music, expansive marble, and exquisite surroundings made me feel like a princess among royalty. However, our discussion was pure earth and spirit, and not at all pompous or trivial.

"Isn't this wonderful?" I said. "Here we are having this great New Age discussion at the Ritz!"

Ivonne raised her water glass in a toast and said, "It shows that nothing's separate. Keep your heart open always, and if you happen to be at the Ritz, well . . ."

We toasted to unlimitedness. After all, who said that spirituality and poverty were synonymous? Didn't the Creator want the very best for us all? And wasn't the Universe absolutely prosperous, expanding, and unlimited? I vowed to reflect the love of the Creator more consistently by adopting a mental and verbal detox program, and to think and speak only love.

As we said goodnight after a European-style long and leisurely dinner, Alex bowed and said to Steven and me, "In'Lakech." In response to our puzzled expressions, Alex explained that the Mayan word (pronounced *In-lak-ESH*) means "I am another you." Similar to the familiar Sanskrit word *Namaste,* In'Lakech is an acknowledgment of our oneness.

Another reason to steadily guard my thoughts, especially about others, the word reminded me. I then recalled a passage from *A Course in Miracles:* "When you meet anyone, remember it is a holy encounter. As you see him, you will see yourself. As you treat him, you will treat yourself. As you think of him, you will think of yourself. Never forget this, for in him, you will find yourself or lose yourself."

✵ ✵ ✵ ✦ ✦ ✦

Chapter 7

12/12,
THE HOLY MOTHER DAY

The Ritz concierge said that the El Rey Mayan ruins were only a 15-minute walk from our hotel. Yet, an hour later, we were still nowhere near our destination. It was December 12, and the angels told me that the number 12, especially when repeated on this date of 12/12, was quite powerful.

The numeral 1 means "Watch your thoughts and only hold thoughts about your true desires, as your thoughts are manifesting instantly right now." And number 2 means "Hold onto faith that your desires are manifesting, even if you can't yet see them. Keep watering the seedlings until they bloom, and don't quit five seconds before the miracle." Together, the 1 and 2 in "12" mean "With faith and focused thought, you can manifest anything rapidly."

It was also Holy Mother Day in Mexico, a feast and celebration in honor of Mother Mary. In Mexico, she's often referred to as "Our Lady of Guadalupe" because of miraculous visions that first occurred in 1531 outside of Mexico City. During this visitation, an image of Our Lady was impressed upon a *tilma* (a piece of cactus cloth). The tilma image still exists today, and several scientists haven't been able to explain its existence.

Signs promised that the El Rey ruins were near, so Steven and I kept walking. The loud traffic prevented us from holding a thoughtful discussion as we'd normally do during a long walk. But as soon as we entered the gates of El Rey, I knew that our efforts had been rewarded.

El Rey's energy was both sweet and powerful, a true blend of feminine yin and masculine yang. Since I'd nearly finished writing the booklet accompanying my *Goddess Guidance Oracle Cards,* I was immersed in goddess energy. I'd been particularly drawn to the Mayan goddess Ixchel (pronounced *EE-shell*). I was attracted to her powerful healing abilities, and also to her water connection. Ixchel is considered the living embodiment of waterfalls, rain, and the water aspect of rainbows. I felt a shared connection with water and Ixchel.

El Rey was a Mayan city in ruins, with only foundations and stone pillars remaining of most of the buildings. Countless iguanas sunned themselves along the rubble, looking like miniature dragons guarding the gates. The iguanas bravely approached Steven and me to have a closer look. Thank goodness I wasn't squeamish around reptiles. In fact, there was something beautiful and majestic about them.

I climbed the steps to a pyramid temple and sat on top of the structure. From my vantage point, I could see an area that appeared to have been used for ceremonies.

I closed my eyes and prayed to the Mother, the feminine spirit of the Creator: "Holy Mother . . . Mary . . . Ixchel . . . Creator Goddess . . . there seems to be so much madness in this world. Please give me a healing message."

A powerful feminine voice broadcast into my mind immediately. It was many voices intertwined, and I saw a vision of a beautiful Mayan queen with a birdlike headdress. It was Ixchel! My heart leapt with joy, and she began speaking:

"Often you view your fellow man with an eye of suspicion, and you feel vulnerable and unsafe. Shroud each situation with a cloak of maternal love. Blanket the earth with the nurturing energy she seeks and so rightly deserves. Use your storehouse of knowledge," she said, making clear that this message was for everyone and not just me, *"to clean up her conditions for the next generation preparing to appear on this planet.*

"Restore also hope in your country [the United States]. *Hope has been debased as being naïve and as a simpleton's acceptance of untruths. Yet hope and faith bathe your soul and quench your body's need for higher vibrational frequencies. Hope is like an iron magnet attracting the dawn of new experiences and adventures such as you would want. Abandon*

your mental dress rehearsals of negative or frightening scenarios, as you will eventually succeed in bringing these into your sphere."

When I asked about the new children, she said, *"The rain forest has been knocked down, but a fresh crop is emerging."* She explained that new growth and life always and perpetually appear, to replace and replenish damage done by previous generations. *"It is the very essence and nature of life,"* Ixchel said matter-of-factly.

I asked, "So I shouldn't be worried about the future of the planet or the new children?"

Ixchel replied, *"Worry never accomplished any good thing, but a plan of action based upon a desire to do good always brings more light into the world."*

Parallel Universes

Then Ixchel said, *"Ask about parallel lives."* So I did.

"Parallel universes existed long before man's advent on the scene of the material landscape. Energetically, they are windows much like your shops' revolving doors, which allow you to shut out one 'reality' in favor of another. You do this through simple decision-making: 'I will live this way, I won't live that way,' and so on.

"The power of the human mind is beyond third-dimensional comprehension, yet you can still tap in to its graces by collectively and individually making blessed decisions. Show your strength through reemerging with this sentient part of yourselves. Make your decision for a clean planet, kindness extended to all children and animals, and so forth.

"So much energy is put into worry, which is a misguided way to pray. Why not instead take calculated risks and make firm, collective group decisions, which will ensure that they are enacted upon?"

Ixchel's words reverberated in my mind all the way back to the hotel. The goddess had emphasized the power of our individual and collective decisions to bring about results, and she said that we too often sit on the sidelines of life, afraid of making the "wrong" decision. Ixchel pointed out that something had to be done to clean up our planet, so we needed to overcome our apathy and indecision.

I thought about the many times I'd made a firm decision and then the universe had rushed to help me. When I was a young mother, for example, money for food and utilities was scarce. One time when I had no idea how I'd feed my sons, I put my foot down to the universe and said, "I need food now!" An hour later at the grocery store, I found a hundred-dollar bill. Another time I received an unexpected check in the mail that exactly covered the utility bills, one day before everything was going to be turned off for lack of payment.

So many times when I got crystal clear about my needs and decisions, magic instantly happened. But when I wavered in indecision, things stayed the same or even worsened. My clarity connected me to the Source.

"This is Source-ery!" I gasped. I had strong feelings and memories of being killed in past lives for the "heresy" of sorcery. Yet, true Source-ery connected us to our Divine power. If we truly were made in the image and likeness of the Creator, then we too possessed the ability to create.

Centuries of religious persecution had brainwashed us into believing that it was wrong to exercise this power. We'd given away our power to "authority figures," without realizing that we're our *own* authority figures! Ixchel's words warmed my heart and mind, as she reminded me of the importance of all of us reclaiming our connection to Source.

It was time for the Sourcer-ers and Sourcer-esses to reawaken!

❊ ▣ ❊

That night at Café Mexicana in the Ritz-Carlton Hotel, three small children danced to a two-woman mariachi band. When the band ended each song, a small blond boy wearing a bright yellow shirt and pants pulled his thumb out of his mouth and exclaimed, "One more song, please!" Each time a song would end, he would utter this phrase.

The band moved away from the boy and his family to play music in another part of the restaurant. "I can't see the song!" the boy said twice to his grandmother, tugging at her sleeve. The woman led the boy to the band, where the two happily danced to the tunes.

I thought of all the Crystal Children I'd met and interviewed during my travels, and how so many had a keen connection to music. Crystal Children often hummed or sang before they began speaking with words. Some of these kids displayed inherent gifts with musical instruments.

The little boy in the Cancún restaurant showed no interest in eating. He simply wanted to follow the band around so that he could listen endlessly to music.

The Alabaster Dragon Upon the Purple Clouds

The next morning, Steven, Alex, Ivonne, and I gathered in a meeting room at the hotel for my daylong workshop on angels. As we walked into the windowless room, I wondered why so many oceanfront hotels didn't have meeting rooms and ballrooms with views. I wondered how I'd withstand a full day of artificial lighting and recirculated air, when the beach was right outside the door.

I went into a semi-trance as I began the workshop, so my earthly concerns faded from view. Alex sat next to me, translating my words into Spanish. His energy was wonderful, and we often looked at each other and wordlessly communicated, since he also received angelic messages during the day.

At my workshops, I let the angels lead the way and tell me what to say, since they know exactly what each audience needs. On this particular day, the angels had me weave teachings about angels in with guided meditations. During the first meditation, I described Archangels Michael and Raphael.

People often ask me if I believe that the archangels are Caucasian, and I tell them that angels don't have race or skin color since they don't have skin. But they do have aura colorings, and Michael's aura has two colors. Immediately next to his body, there's a definite golden glow, then layered above the golden light is an electric purple coloring mixed with cobalt blue. Many people report seeing flashes of bright purple or blue light, which is a sign that Michael is near.

Archangel Raphael, who oversees physical healings and healers, isn't as tall as Michael. He has a large, muscular chest and short, thick legs. Raphael's aura is bright emerald green, which lends an otherworldly appearance to him. Raphael uses his index finger and the green light in his healing and teaching work, which includes helping healers, answering prayers for physical healings, working alongside Jesus and other ascended masters, eradicating addictions, finding lost pets, helping travelers during their trips, and taking care of animals.

After describing Michael and Raphael, I told the audience members, "Envision these archangels standing in front of you and lovingly embracing you. See and feel the archangels carrying you Heavenward. You are safe, loved, and protected and can return to Earth whenever you like.

"Michael and Raphael are carrying you to a large, beautiful purple cloud in the sky, where the vibrational frequency is much higher. This cloud lifts your spirits and opens new avenues for you and your life."

My meditations constantly change and evolve, since the angels always show me new visions to describe. I journey along with the audience during each meditation, and sometimes I can't recall what I saw or said afterward because I'm in an altered state of consciousness.

This meditation, though, was unforgettable because in the purple clouds I saw a magnificent snow-white dragon with purple tufts of fur around his head. I shared this vision privately with Alex during the first workshop break. "What did he look like?" my new friend asked.

When I described the dragon, Alex exclaimed, "That's *my* dragon! His name is Ashtorg, and he works with Quetzalcoatl, the supreme Mayan deity. Quetzalcoatl is the Mayan god of medicine, healing, and fertility, and he's strongly associated with the planet Venus."

I knew what was happening: The dragon had come to help me lose my fear and distrust of such creatures. I'd met many dragons during my psychic readings, as several of my clients had them as spirit guides. Some of them were angelic and even petlike, but too many of my clients had dragon attachments with negative consequences. In those instances, the dragon drained energy from the client and brought about negativity. For instance, one woman's dragon came equipped with an ever-raining black cloud that created the experience of steady bad luck for her, so I banished it. Another woman's dragon had hooked talons that bore into her shoulders, causing pain until I shooed the beast away.

The inconsistency of dragons left me with an unpleasant taste for, and distrust of, them. Once while giving a book signing, I asked the store owner to move two large dragon statues that seemed to be staring at me. As he moved them, one statue caught on an angel statue, causing it to fall and shatter into bits. This fueled my prejudice even further.

Yet here in Mayan territory, the dragon was considered heroic and virtuous. And Alex was telling me that my Mayan astrological sign was a dragon. I was open-minded enough to take another look at these creatures. I knew that there were some beautiful and loving ones, but how could I avoid the other sort? Then I thought of the many fairy tales in which dragons both protected and abducted fair maidens. Was there a goddess/dragon connection?

I learned that many cultures recognize the dragon as a bridge between Heaven and Earth. For instance, the Babylonians regarded a dragon named Tiamat as the Mother Goddess of their deities. Tiamat existed before the world's creation, and she originated from the waters. Her tail extended to Heaven, and her body reached the earth. Archaeological images of Tiamat portray her as a mermaid, or a beautiful woman with a dragon tail.

The Aztecs revered Itzpapalotl, a dragon goddess with butterfly wings that symbolize her ability to positively transform. Itzpapalotl is a creation and fertility goddess. Chinese creation stories credit the dragon goddess, Nu-Kua, as fashioning the earth's first humans out of clay. Nu-Kua then breathed Divine life force into the humans.

Ancient Africans contended that the androgynous dragon Aido Hwedo was the first created being on Earth. They believe that Aido Hwedo's dung formed the first mountains, and the dragon supports the earth with its tail.

In addition, the Japanese sea goddess, Benten, rides upon a dragon as she delivers blessings and protection to people. The stories of dragons in worldwide spiritual beliefs are so ancient and consistent with each other that one begins to wonder: Were dragons physical creatures on the planet who are now extinct? How else could cultures around the globe have described the same thing?

And the fact that so many cultures associate dragons with both creation and water intrigued me. Could this be a fragmented memory of our own watery origins? Could the dragons actually be a version of a dolphin, manatee, or other water creature connected with human creation?

As I looked at ancient paintings of dragon Creator goddesses, I was struck by how they resembled mermaids. In India, for instance, the Nagas of the Waters are beautiful half-humans with coiled lower bodies who live in the sea. Most have the head and upper torso of a woman, with a long green tail that could be either a dragon or a fish tail.

Many cultures believe in amphibious Creator gods and goddesses. In the Syrian culture, a mermaid goddess named Atargatis was said to be the world's Creator. The Chinese Creator deities, Fu-Hsi and Nu Kua, are a merman and mermaid, respectively. Another amphibious Creator god named Oannes brought civilization to the Babylonians. The African Dogon tribe say that they were created by amphibious beings called the Nommos from the star Sirius (which they describe in perfect detail, despite their lack of telescopes or astronomical education). Even Isis and Osiris have been illustrated with fish tails in ancient Egypt.

Why would so many cultures feature mermaid-like beings in their creation stories, unless some kernel of truth supported these accounts? I vowed to discover more.

※ ※ ※ ※ ※ ※

He waved his hand and scoffed, "We Mayans have no connection to the stars or ETs. We're down-to-earth people who believe that we were manifested from four androgynous grandparents who came from a pantheon of gods."

I suspected that other Mayan shamans might have differing opinions about the topic, but I kept my vow of open-mindedness as Manuel continued to explain the Mayan history of creation: "Much of the story of Creation is written in our sacred book, *Popol Vuh*. Mayans believe that in the beginning was darkness, and life came out of the sea, and then light followed. Life came from four Creator Mothers from the water who married gods. The first Creator Mother was *Cahá-Paluna*, whose name means 'standing water falling from above.' The Creator Mothers who followed were *Chomiha*, meaning 'beautiful, chosen water'; *Tzununihá*, which translates into 'water of hummingbirds'; and *Caquixahá*, meaning 'water of the macaw.'"

I told Manuel about my fascination with mermaids and the idea that we'd all sprung from the sea, and he said, "Mayans believe that all life came from the ocean. Water is used in sacred rituals. In fact, the name Itzá, which is the suffix of the civilization we're traveling to today, means 'the well of the water sorcerers.'"

The Mayans performed ceremonies at the large sacred well, or *cenote*, at Chichén Itzá. The phrase "water sorcerers" intrigued me. Did the Mayans perform healings and magical manifestations with water? It was said that water sorcerers worked with elementals such as sprites and undines, who carried out the sorcerers' requests.

I asked about Mayan spirituality, and Manuel replied, "The Mayan philosophy is to treat others as you would want them to treat you. We [humankind] once had the ability to do what God and the gods can do, such as levitation, but we lost it because we began eating meat and getting intoxicated. Once you lose your God-abilities, it's difficult to get them back. This is not so much a punishment as it is a result of lowering your energy with meat and alcohol."

We stopped our car at a rest stop, and Ivonne's van, which had been following us, did the same. As we stepped out of our car, a large bright yellow-and-orange butterfly flew inside our car. "The butterfly is preparing you for transformation and clearing the car," Ivonne said to me. Then Ivonne asked her small daughter to talk with the butterfly and ask it to leave the car, which it promptly did.

The Pyramid

Even though I'd seen photos and paintings of the famous pyramid of Chichén Itzá, I was unprepared for its majestic size and beauty upon seeing it in person.

"The El Castillo pyramid is composed of an inner and an outer building," Manuel explained. "In Mayan culture, science and religion were the same, so the pyramids were built according to mathematical formulas around the Mayan calendar.

"The Mayans used two calendar systems, one with 260 days, called the Tzolkin, and the other with 365 days, called the Haab. The Tzolkin has a feminine energy, as it's tied in with the cycles of pregnancy, the moon, and Venus. You might call it a calendar of the goddess.

"After all, 260 days is approximately the number of days of gestation, roughly corresponding to nine moon cycles. The moon and the planet Venus are long associated with the goddess and the feminine spirit, so it's also interesting that the Mayan Tzolkin calendar corresponds to Venus's cycles. The planet moves from being the morning star to the evening star approximately every 260 days. Venus's distance from the earth is just shy of 260 million kilometers as well.

"In contrast, the 365-day Haab calendar is built upon solar cycles, like the Gregorian calendar used in much of the world. So it's a more masculine energy. Many Mayan structures use architectural symbolism based on both the Tzolkin and the Haab calendars, fusing and intersecting feminine and masculine energies."

Manuel explained that the pyramid's interior has 65 steps on each of its four sides, which equals 260. There are 91 steps on each of its four exterior sides, which adds up to 364. This is also based upon 91 days separating each solstice. When you count the one large top step, you have 365. So, the pyramid itself is a perfect balance of both Mayan calendars, with the feminine interior and the masculine exterior.

"The Mayan is a matriarchal society, and Mexico continues this tradition," Manuel said as he stepped away from the pyramid.

Then he stopped and said to Steven and me, "Listen to this!" Manuel clapped his hands, and the echo sounded just like a screeching eagle.

While Steven and Manuel explored the grounds, I climbed partway up the pyramid and sat on a step. The sun was setting, and I was grateful for the cool shade after the very hot day. A man climbing down the steps behind me said to his wife, "Fear is only in the mind. It's not real." I saw his wife scooting down the pyramid using her hands, sitting on each step, while her husband walked upright down the steps. Those pyramid steps were very steep, especially with no handrails!

I closed my eyes and silently called upon Ixchel and her sister Ixtab. "Come to me now, please! Ancient goddesses on high, please give me a message for my own health and growth, as well as for those who read it."

Instantly their words came through: *"With the distribution of wealth being seen as uneven, no one can succeed or properly survive. The underpinning of a successful civilization is one of plenty for all. The Mayan/Toltec ancestry recognized royalty as spirit and wisdom alone, and not based upon wealth. No one strived to get ahead of others. They held their place in the world as one of cooperation, and not of supremacy or conquering. They gave places upon the earth their names, but they never claimed* ownership *of Earth. They considered Earth and the stars as their teachers and not as their property.*

"There was mutual respect extended both to *nature and* from *nature. Both provided for the other. For instance, if there was a fire, then the underbrush was allowed to grow again before it was harvested. And so it is with mankind: total respect for natural cycles, for the equality of all, for the feelings of all, and for the providership of life."*

The goddesses then showed me a vision of a purple-and-green symbol and told me to draw it in my notebook. I drew a four-pointed green star of Venus, and a tightly coiled serpent in a circle behind Venus. It looked like a Celtic cross, except for the many coils of the circles behind it. It reminded me of the ancient relics from India depicting their mermaid Creator goddesses, with the image of a woman in the center of a coiled spiral tail. The goddesses said to me, *"Venus represents healing, femininity, and goddess. The purple serpent spiral represents Earth."*

I felt a lot of energy in my head, and excitement mixed with warm love in my heart. I could feel Steven coming up behind me. I turned, and he was indeed there. I walked down the pyramid with him to meet Alex, Ivonne, Manuel, and the children.

Alex asked, "Did you see the serpent on the pyramid?" At first I thought he'd seen the same vision of Venus with the purple serpent. But as I followed his outstretched index finger, I saw that there were serpents carved into each side of the pyramid.

"And on each spring and autumn equinox, the sun casts a shadow that looks exactly like a feathered serpent down the steps of the pyramid," Manuel added. The pyramid architects were truly astronomers, mathematicians, and sorcerers.

Manuel then took me to a temple near the pyramid. He pointed to a relief carving in the stone building. "That's Venus," he said. My jaw dropped, as the carving looked identical to my vision on the pyramid! "Venus is shown with four points because it passes in front of the sun four times each year. The light of the Venus star shines on this exact spot every 52 years using the Mayan Haab calendar of 365 days," Manuel explained. "That's every five Calendar Rounds, which is the term for a round Mayan calendar carved with marks indicating every 52 years. The path of Venus is traced on the Calendar Round connecting those five points, until its five successions create a five-pointed star."

Ivonne announced that we were going to lunch at a nearby café with another Mayan shaman named Adalberto Rivera. Manuel bid us farewell, and at 6:05 P.M., our two vehicles pulled out of the Chichén Itzá parking lot to have lunch. In Mexico, everything's relaxed, so meals are held . . . well, whenever it works out.

The Rainbow Child

We drove to a quaint roadside café. *This is definitely no tourist-trap restaurant,* I thought, looking at the authentic details mimicked by chain Mexican restaurants. Usually I could find vegetarian and vegan food choices anywhere, but this place was challenging. We were eating at an outside buffet, and the browned and shriveled fruits and vegetables looked like they'd soaked up a little too much heat during the day. When I asked the owner for papaya, I was handed a whole fruit, a knife, and a plate.

Other people eating at the café sat next to us on the long benches in the adjacent courtyard. A small boy sat across from me, staring at me intently with long-eyelashed eyes. His steady, loving gaze signaled that he was one of the new children. Yet this boy was different from the Crystal Children I'd met on my journeys. His energy seemed significantly higher. *"He's a Rainbow Child,"* I heard whispered in my right ear, and my body broke out in goose bumps.

His mother explained that little Jose Luis was two years old and would turn three on March 3, which she quickly pointed out was the date of 3/3.

Jose continued to stare at me, and finally he pointed to himself and said in Spanish, "I am a Boy Wizard."

My mouth must have dropped open, because his mother explained that Jose was quite psychic. "Jose told his older sister that she was once a ballerina, although she'd never spoken of the ballet she'd done before he was born."

Unlike a Crystal Child, Jose seemed more comfortable with strangers and more apt to talk. I thought of the Crystal and Indigo Children I'd met during my travels and some of their distinguishing characteristics.

For example, Indigo Children have a very masculine energy, with warrior traits of willfulness and natural leadership skills. Indigos are sensitive to chemicals, including their own body chemistry. They can also detect dishonesty instantly, and they trust their gut feelings when sizing up someone's character and integrity. You can't lie to an Indigo, that's for sure. In fact, their groups' soul purpose is to rid the planet of corruption and greed, and usher in cooperation and integrity.

This lofty mission is fueled by the Indigos' anger and angst. It's important not to squelch the Indigos' anger, but to teach them how to manage it constructively. Indigos also need outlets for their great energy, such as cardiovascular exercise and artistic projects. Without such outlets, Indigos have difficulties that often result in a mislabeled ADHD diagnosis.

The next generation of highly sensitive youths are called Crystal Children. Unlike the Indigos, Crystals are calm, sweet, and quiet; and their energy is very feminine. In fact, they're so quiet that they're often misdiagnosed as having autism or Asperger's Syndrome. Crystal Children prefer to communicate telepathically or through music, which are better ways for them to convey deep and complex feelings than talking.

Crystal Children have strong connections to nature, and they need to be outdoors regularly. They also develop close bonds with domestic and wild animals. They're even more sensitive to chemicals than Indigos, so Crystal Children usually require organic diets, and special laundry soap and fabrics to avoid allergic reactions.

Rainbow Children are the next vibrational level following the generation of Crystal Children. Rainbows have perfectly balanced male and female energy. Rainbows are like "little Buddhas," both wise and serene. They're more interested in giving than receiving. Because Rainbow Children have never before incarnated, they don't have earthly karma to work out. Therefore, they only select harmonious, functional families in which to be born.

Rainbows are just now beginning to populate the planet. The largest influx of Indigos was born between 1975 and 1995 (although some were born before and after those years). The Crystal generation now has its foothold, and new Crystals will continue to be born through 2015. Interestingly, as the Mayan calendar flips to its end, the Rainbow Children will begin their reign upon the planet.

The Mysteries of Chichén Itzá

Adalberto Rivera and his wife arrived at the café. As Ivonne introduced us, I marveled at the couple's physical and energetic attractiveness. The couple both wore crisp white-gauze clothing with white hats, which set off their sun-browned skin. Adalberto was soft-spoken, and his wife barely uttered a word during our meeting, yet their energy communicated excitement for their work studying Mayan ruins, particularly Chichén Itzá, which was near their home.

Adalberto is the author of *The Mysteries of Chichén Itzá,* considered to be the first guide to the esoteric functions of its temples and pyramids. He's also one of the main aficionados of the scientific and religious aspects of the Mayan culture worldwide. One of his most important discoveries is the projection of "The Serpent of Shadow" during the precession on the equinox. This phenomenon attracts thousands of visitors from around the world every year.

Adalberto handed me a smooth brown stone that sent shock waves into my hand with its electric energy. I heard a voice repeatedly say about the stone: *"Ancient Mayan ritual."* In a hushed whisper so other restaurant patrons wouldn't overhear, Adalberto explained that the stone was from the Pleiades, where people from the Chichén Itzá region originated from. "Itzá is very connected to the Pleiades, and the Pleiadeans hover above Chichén Itzá every night. The Milky Way crosses its path. I also believe that the bees in this area are from the Pleiades because of their uniqueness— they don't have stomachs, and their honey is very different and extremely healing."

Adalberto was a wealth of knowledge. He acknowledged that his teachings were controversial, but he said they were based on years of living near the celebrated ruins and studying them closely. He explained that the energy veins called "ley lines" under Chichén Itzá's observatory are serpent lines (meaning that they curve in S patterns, as opposed to straight lines) connected to Egypt. As I do, Adalberto believes that the wisdom of the Mayans descended straight from Atlantis and Egypt.

One of Adalberto's missions is to dispel beliefs that the Mayans conducted sacrifices and beheadings. These rumors are based on sculptures and etched drawings on Mayan ruins, including Chichén Itzá. Adalberto believes the drawings of decapitations are symbolic.

"A decapitation in the Mayan spiritual sense means transitioning from processing information in your head, and instead focusing on your gut feelings and listening to the intuition in your gut," he said.

Ivonne chimed in, readily agreeing with Adalberto. "In Chichén, there were never killings. All was a symbolism of the Divine. The drawings of the heart out of the body represent offering the heart to existence. The figures showing men with their heads off represent surrendering the ego."

Adalberto also said that the Mayan animals frequently used in temple structures and artwork are symbolic, too. "The jaguar symbolizes the ego, the eagle is symbolic of the heart and spirit, and the serpent is a symbol of energy and philosophy," he explained.

We spoke with Adalberto and his wife until the restaurant closed late that evening. We probably could have continued talking all night, but we had to catch an early flight home the next morning.

* * * * * *

Chapter 9

HEALING FROM THE INSIDE OUT

A major storm pummeled Southern California on Christmas Day. As I sat in my living room watching the wind whip through the trees with such force that they bent sideways, I was frightened for them. Then I heard the angels say, *"The wind is a natural way to loosen and release dead leaves and branches, just as emotional and life-situation storms are opportunities for humans to release 'deadwood' and anything needing to be swept away."*

The next morning, Steven and I awoke to a sunny blue sky. The storm had washed away the smog, and everything looked sparkling new.

"Look!" He pointed to the balcony bannister railing outside our bedroom window. There stood a chubby black bird sporting a white chest. "She's looking at us!" Steven exclaimed. And there it was: a deliberate stare from a species of bird I'd never seen before.

As we backed out of our driveway later that day, I said, "Look, there's the white-breasted bird again!" The bird perched on our railing far from the bird feeder popular with neighborhood sparrows, doves, and crows. The fact that this bird was acting very strangely was definitely a sign.

"White breast," my husband reflected. "What does the color white mean?"

"Protection," I said. Steven and I both sat in silent meditation during the drive, pondering the bird and its message. I thought of the symbolism of its breast. So many times I'd felt as if I were breast-feeding certain people, and so many times I'd given and given while feeling resentful, obliged, and guilty. At those times, I wasn't offering a true gift—I was giving bitter, sour milk. I also wasn't being authentic, as Archangel Michael had counseled me to be.

So I silently told my angels, "I undo this, and ask that all effects of errors in my thinking be undone in all directions of time." I forgave and asked forgiveness from everyone whom I perceived as being pushy. I was happy to help sweet, kind people who needed my assistance—my difficulty was with those who seemed to feel entitled to my endless help, and they were the ones who became upset when I drew boundaries on my time and energy and said no. They were the ones I needed to forgive and let go of.

"I now only attract sweet, considerate, and grateful people into my life," I affirmed.

That night, Shannon Kennedy, the Ayurvedic medical doctor, gave me a massage. Shannon pressed my arm backwards to loosen my shoulder socket and muscles, and I felt some pain.

Then I saw him clearly: a golden dragon stood over the shoulder Shannon was working on. He had wings and was the color of a golden Labrador retriever. He hissed threateningly at Shannon to protect me from harm, his mouth open and baring large teeth. I'd never met this animal spirit guide before!

I asked him his name, and when he said "Dino," like the *Flintstones* dinosaur, I laughed! He was entirely lovable, like a protective pet dog, and only fierce toward Shannon because he thought she was hurting me. Mentally, I assured Dino that I was okay and that Shannon was merely loosening my muscles. Satisfied that I was safe, Dino retreated.

Had Dino always been there and only come forward because of my recent open-mindedness toward dragons? Or was he a new spirit guide who'd come to protect me, as my work continued to take me further out into the world?

As Shannon worked on my shoulder, I saw another being enter the room. This time it was a familiar visitor from the spirit world: Merlin, the magical Celtic wizard who also shape-shifts across time to become Hermes, the great Atlantean and Grecian healer; and also Thoth, the Egyptian alchemist and scribe.

Merlin, in his full wizard regalia, pointed a rose quartz crystal wand toward my shoulder. Light and energy streamed out of his wand, and I felt flushed with warmth. Just then my shoulder popped into place and instantly healed with no further trouble

The Unedited Course

During my travels, a man gave me a copy of the Hugh Lynn Cayce version of *A Course in Miracles*. I'd studied the edited *Course* for several years, completely reading the text and teacher's manual nearly a dozen times.

I got in touch with the distributor of the Hugh Lynn Cayce version, also known as the *Jesus Course in Miracles*. They told me the story of this version:

The scribes of the *Course*, Helen Schucman and Bill Thetford, worked with an editor to distill the extremely long original text (sometimes called the *Urtext*) into a shorter version. They also deleted personal comments that Jesus made to Bill and Helen.

An edited version was sent to Hugh Lynn Cayce, grandson of the famed psychic Edgar Cayce. Hugh put the version in the public library at the Cayce Association for Research and Enlightenment in Virginia Beach. Someone found and began distributing the Hugh Lynne Cayce version of the *Course*. In the meantime, a third version had been published worldwide by Viking Press and the Foundation for Inner Peace. This version was edited even more than the Hugh Lynn Cayce version.

The publishers of the *Course* filed a lawsuit against the distributors of the Hugh Lynn Cayce version. The judge ruled that since the Hugh Lynn Cayce version was freely distributed by its authors, it couldn't be copyrighted.

During the copyright dispute, I was named an expert witness since I was a longtime student of the *Course,* a former psychotherapist (like Helen and Bill), and an author of channeled books. As a party to the lawsuit, I received a photocopy of the *Urtext,* or the original, unedited version of *A Course in Miracles*. I was naturally excited, but the immense size of the text (several hundred pages of typewritten and handwritten material) was daunting. The huge tome sat in my office for years.

Writing and speaking my intentions aloud to a group of trusted friends on New Year's Eve always helps me achieve my desires, especially when I'm procrastinating. So, on that New Year's Eve, Steven and I gathered at the house of Chris and Becky Prelitz (she's the co-author of my book *Eating in the Light*), along with Lynnette, Judith Lukomski (co-author of *Crystal Therapy*), and a few other close friends.

We sat in a circle and read our written intentions for the forthcoming year aloud. One of my intentions was to read the unedited *Course in Miracles* from front to back, a few pages at a time each day. A second intention was to meet the Dalai Lama. Another was to move back to the beach, as I wanted to hear the ocean surf again (we lived on a hill with a spectacular ocean view, but no crashing-surf sounds).

As I read each intention, I felt their inevitability in my gut. I knew that they were going to happen, and I didn't worry how they'd manifest. I'd learned to surrender any need I had to control or predict how the universe would deliver my desires. This was similar to my decision to never use my psychic abilities to discern the contents of my birthday or Christmas gifts. It was much more fun to sit back and let myself be surprised!

So, on New Year's Day, I placed the large box with the unedited *Course in Miracles* next to my bed and began reading. Since I was very familiar with both the Hugh Lynn Cayce and the edited standard versions of the *Course,* I was struck by the differences in the unedited version.

For those unfamiliar with the *Course,* it's a dictated book that Helen Schucman received in the 1960s. The book is divided into sections, with the largest being the *Text,* in which Jesus teaches Helen to heal her mind from fear, anger, and guilt.

Many people, myself included, have complained that the standard *Course* is written in staccato, stilted language, making it difficult reading. I could only digest a couple of pages at a time.

The Hugh Lynn Cayce version was more of a narrative, making it easier to read. It also used fewer traditional Christian terms. Most surprising to me was when Jesus used the phrase "spiritual sight" in his original dictation to Helen. In the edited version, "Holy Spirit" was substituted for "spiritual sight." I believe that Jesus was discussing our inner Divine-guidance abilities whenever he talked about spiritual sight in the original *Course.*

The *Urtext* (the completely unedited version of the *Course*) was an entirely different experience, almost in a different league from the edited *Course*. It was like reading a conversation with Jesus! I understood why some of the original text had been deleted, as it contained highly personal topics. It also used psychoanalytic terms to describe Helen's relationship with Bill. Someone unfamiliar with psychoanalysis could misinterpret this discussion, so it seemed only fitting that it had been stricken from the *Course's* two edited versions.

But other parts of the *Course* felt akin to reading *The Dead Sea Scrolls* or some other hidden sacred writings. I immediately wanted to show it to everyone. But I remembered the legal document I'd signed promising not to distribute this version of the *Course*. So I was happy to see bootlegged downloadable copies of the *Urtext* freely available on the Web to anyone who typed the word *Urtext* into an Internet search engine.

I was thrilled to read about priestesses, Atlantis, and Edgar Cayce's work in the original *Course*. I also drank in Jesus' words about the origination of time. He said that humans created time when they thought God's perfection could be, and needed to be, improved upon. This desire for improvement created past, present, and future so that there would be a basis of comparison to notice improvement. As soon as we realize that everything is perfect now, the need for time will be abolished.

The bulk of the unedited text discusses why and how to control your thoughts away from judgments. As in the edited *Course*, Jesus emphasizes our oneness with each other. If I judge you, then I'm really judging myself. My ego lower-self is the basis of all fear and judgment. Yet I don't want to own or acknowledge my ego-traits, so I project them onto you. Everything I judge in you is something within myself that I don't want to face.

One phrase in particular struck me so profoundly that I wrote it on a separate piece of paper and put it on my nightstand, so I could meditate on it before and after sleep:

"You have no idea of the tremendous release and deep peace that comes from meeting yourself and your brother totally without judgment."

Since you and everyone else are perfect Holy children of God, judging yourself or others is without meaning, and a waste of time that robs you of your spiritual gifts and power. A related phrase I also copied and meditated upon is:

"Miracle working entails a full realization of the power of thought, and a real avoidance of miscreation."

Miscreation occurs whenever we believe that we're separate from God, love, or each other. It takes vigilance to constantly perceive each other as one, yet we regain our miraculous spiritual power by doing so.

I wondered: Is it possible to truly see ourselves as one? Is it possible to have a mind without judgment? Is it wise to become so pure, so sensitive?

Would this mean no more gossipy media like *People* magazine or the E! channel? Being entirely nonjudgmental requires total commitment, especially since celebrity gossip is such a social lubricant. How would our lives change if we adopted nonjudgmental outlooks?

Then I remembered the difference between judgment and discernment: An example of judgment is when I use my mind to label something or someone as "good" or "bad." Discernment is when my gut feelings guide me toward or away from a person or situation. Discernment is a healthy and natural process using the "Law of Attraction," the energy force that draws similar people or experiences to us.

I realized that I was judging myself for being judgmental! I heard a voice counseling me: *"Have loving compassion for yourself for projecting fears. The fears are unreal and irrelevant, and unworthy of your time, energy, or obsession. They are like a bad movie you once saw. Let them go—forget about them."*

The *Song of Prayer* section of the *Urtext* says that guilt creates feelings and beliefs in scarcity and lack. When we let go of guilt, we're never in scarcity or lack again.

That makes so much sense, but how can we let go of guilt? According to the *Song of Prayer*, we're always praying. *What am I praying for?* is the question. *And how am I praying? Is there underlying guilt in my prayers?*

Whenever I say, "Please help me with this!" I realized that this prayer assumes lack and a need for help. Isn't it true that I, like all children of God, am truly guiltless? But the *feeling* of guilt came from somewhere, so I wanted to know if it's possible to be completely free of guilt.

Healing from Guilt

I'd read the *Urtext* for several days straight, and my phone messages were accumulating. I decided to take the morning to return calls. Reading the *Course* made me extra-aware of my thoughts and feelings.

After speaking with three different friends on the phone, my body and mind were tense and upset. Each friend had relayed their troubles to me, complete with concerns about their fears, worries, and issues.

That's when it hit me: My body believed that my friends' troubles were *my own!* My mind and body thought I had problems, even though my life was (and still is) virtually trouble free. And since I'm *one* with my friends, it's essential that I see them as problem free, too. I can hold compassion for their fears, but I can't buy into their reality.

True healing comes from seeing only the truth in yourself and others. Seeing this truth cancels out others' errors that they're holding concerning themselves. When you judge someone, you then see them as separate from yourself. This makes you feel afraid because you then can't see and know that God created both of you, as one with each other. The basis of fear is believing that we're separate from God, and we're self-created. Deep down, we fear that we're alone, unprotected, and unprepared. There's also a deep-seated fear of God's punishment for usurping his role and power. Plus, there's the insecurity of being unaware of God's love and gifts.

I realized the high price of holding negative thoughts and judgments about another person: Doing so put me into separation, which the *Song of Prayer* says is the basis of all guilt. Guilt is the cause of pain and painful experiences. So I prayed: "Please let me realize the negative judgments I make about myself and others, and to 'choose my battles' carefully. It's too high a price to randomly judge people."

The *Urtext* says that the only meaningful prayer is for forgiveness, because it lifts the veil of recognition that we already have everything we need and want. Forgiveness is the antidote for guilt. Even if we're already forgiven, we need to recognize and feel that fact in order to release guilt's grip.

I thought of the guilty struggles I, and other healers, go through in setting boundaries with our clients and friends. In addition to my "draining" friend Andrea, I'd endured a painful "divorce" from another female friend who couldn't seem to have a two-way friendship with me. Instead, she only wanted me to listen to her and give her free readings. And with my increasing time demands involving traveling and writing, I had to decline offers to give workshops and readings. This upset people who really wanted my attention. Because I'm someone who wishes everyone could be happy, I disliked disappointing them.

Once again, the *Urtext* provided me with solace in a section where Jesus discusses the work of the famed trance medium Edgar Cayce. Jesus clearly said that Cayce erred by saying yes to everyone's requests for his help. Jesus said that he should have said no more often, and that Cayce hurt his body through overwork. Jesus explained that he himself didn't say yes to everyone, because he chose to treat himself with love. Jesus said that Cayce was coming from his ego by never declining anyone's request for help, because the ego believes that it's special.

Well, that certainly eased my mind! Throughout my entire life, I'd always assumed that Jesus gave help endlessly, so my saying no invariably triggered guilt. I breathed a deep sigh of relief upon reading Jesus' comforting advice. Saying no was treating myself with love. Saying yes without boundaries was an ego device built on the false belief that my help was special, so I owed it to the other person to give it to them . . . even if I was exhausted or busy.

Jesus summarized the steps necessary to take prior to healing sessions in a very simple way. My paraphrasing of his steps is:

1. Recognize the importance of the power of thought.

2. Know that everyone involved in the healing is equal, including Jesus.

3. No one is the "healer" or the "patient." Lose those terms.

4 Be assured that everyone desires to release errors in thinking.

5. During a healing, both person's minds will shift to a consciousness of love. This is when healing occurs.

Putting Love into Action

I'd been on a gossip diet, avoiding shows and magazines that judged celebrities. Instead, I watched DVDs related to spiritual topics, especially while exercising. The angels explained that when we exercise, deep breathing increases sensitivity to energy. We must be cautious what we're watching, reading, or listening to while we're exercising.

I felt a huge difference in my level of peacefulness. I'd also continued what I now call "The Archangel Michael Detox Diet," which consisted of a morning smoothie blended with organic juice, fruit, soy protein powder, and super green powder. I'd also been avoiding sulfite-containing foods and beverages. As I mentioned earlier, the result was that I'd lost nearly 45 pounds. But the biggest benefit was my new sense of calmness and peace, an overall feeling of being grounded and secure.

One night Steven and I stepped outside to watch Venus high and bright in the sky, next to the waxing crescent moon. I said, "Look at all that goddess energy. The moon and Venus are so close together and so bright and visible. And Mars is so far from them, like a gathering of women with the man withdrawn and isolated."

"Yes," my husband agreed, "but Mars is nightly drawing closer to Venus, and she's also coming in his direction."

The next day, Steven and I had a telephone appointment with a Sedona astrologer named Sao. "Your chart shows that one of your soul purposes is to bring forward the mastery of the mystery of Venus and Mars," he told me. "I'd like to see you meditate on this purpose. Really call upon your ancestral spirits to help you understand the mysteries of Venus and Mars for yourself and others."

At sunset, Steven and I went to the beach and sat upon the "manifestation rocks," a large group of quartz granite rocks jutting out into the ocean near Mountain Street in Laguna Beach. The rocks have two naturally formed thrones. These were the rocks I'd sat upon while praying to meet my soul mate. Soon after, I was guided to attend yoga classes, where I met my childhood crush, Steven, who is now my husband.

As he and I sat on the rocks now, I called upon my ancestors, angels, and guides to help me master the mysteries of Venus and Mars. As a Taurus, Venus was already my guiding planet, and I'd always felt a strong connection to the morning and evening star. The study of Mars would involve learning to balance the masculine and feminine energies, which each represented.

Like many people, I knew that the goddess energy was emerging at the perfect time. We'd experimented with a monopoly of male patriarchal leaders, only to experience crowded cities, wars, and pollution. Unlike the goddess movement of the 1980s and '90s, there was no need to hold negative views about men. Male-bashing wouldn't help the planet to heal.

What was needed was a balance of both masculine and feminine energy—with women in leadership positions being respected and working harmoniously with male leaders, with each gender honoring the other like a healthy marriage.

＊ ▣ ＊

That night I awoke from a dream about three crystals. Upon awakening, a voice spoke the name of a green crystal called "aventurine." I woke up feeling that I needed this stone.

I asked Judith about aventurine, and she explained, "It's a stone about balancing the Divine feminine and masculine." She brought me a beautiful heart-shaped green aventurine crystal to help with my Divine purpose of balancing male and female within me, and also to teach goddess work incorporating a positive attitude toward men.

already perfect just as you are, and there's nothing you need to fix or change about the true you who's one with the Creator. But in the illusion where we seem to be separate beings, chaos and confusion can sometimes appear. And there may be something— some behavior, habit, or attitude—that stands in the way of remembering who you are."

It felt so great to help audience members remember how equally special and loved they all were. I could feel joy, love, and inner warmth as I taught the principles. *Maybe this is how I'm going to heal the burnout of traveling.*

What a contrast to how I felt on the plane ride home. For some reason, I bought some fashion and gossip magazines at the airport, each one dishing about celebrities. I was resisting reading the *Urtext*, seeing it as dry and work-related material. Yet, looking back on the incident, I realize how my focus on those magazines attracted a most unpleasant situation and an opportunity for growth.

On the big 767 American Airlines jet from Miami to Los Angeles, the flight attendant asked if we'd lower our window shades for better viewing of the movie (*Runaway Jury,* with John Cusack). I kept my shade open by three inches to illuminate my reading and enjoy the sunshine and views.

The movie began, and Steven put on his headphones to watch it. A large man got out of his seat, as if he were going to the restroom. Then he stopped and stood right in front of Steven in the aisle, blocking him from seeing the movie. I tapped the man with my magazine to get his attention. He loudly announced he was purposely blocking the movie because the light from my window bothered him.

Steven and the man exchanged words, and I covered my ears as a shield from the anger energy. Stunned by the sudden attack, I lowered my window shade and began crying. Steven held me until I stopped. We spoke with a flight attendant, who seemed distant and too harried to get involved in our plight. Through tears, I joked, "Maybe she's not a 'plight attendant.'"

Needing some spiritual psychotherapy, I pulled out the *Urtext* manuscript. Naturally, the first page I turned to revealed the words I needed to read: "They attack because they believe they are deprived."

In this incident, I believed that I was being deprived of sunlight, the tall man thought he was being deprived of darkness for the in-flight movie, and Steven thought the tall man's head was depriving him of seeing the movie. We all believed we were being deprived, so we attacked.

The *Urtext's* next sentence was: "But you cannot lose anything unless you do not value it and therefore do not want it."

From a spiritual standpoint, attack is impossible because nothing real can be threatened or harmed. Steven and I smiled at each other, and I took a nap with my head leaning against his shoulder as he enjoyed the rest of the movie—obstruction free.

Understanding the Ego

My *Urtext* studies made me extra-aware of my ego and shadows. I tried to observe these tendencies within myself honestly and with compassion. Whenever I found myself judging another, I immediately looked inward to see what was within myself that I was seeing in the other person.

I realized that the ego was a deep combination of guilt and fear. In fact, since the word *ego* is often misunderstood, we could even change its name to *gaf,* to stand for:

Guilt
And
Fear

Since *gaffe* is a synonym for *mistake,* "gaf" is an appropriate play on words. After all, the ego is always mistaken.

Once Steven and I returned home from the Caribbean, I spent time with a woman who felt guilt as a result of family issues. Each time I spoke with her, I realized that I was absorbing her guilty feelings, and ended up feeling uncomfortable by the end of our conversations!

One time after I'd been with this woman, I came home to find Steven depressed. The guilt I'd already absorbed from my girlfriend was compounded by my husband's mood, as if his depression was my fault. I meditated, and realized that I was focusing on his ego, which was unreal. I instead focused on his true self. This higher focus gave Steven the loving support he needed. He soon gained insight into the reason behind his depression, and his normally cheerful mood returned.

When I'd met with my friend earlier, I'd affirmed her guilt as being real. And what I saw in her (and others), I manifested within myself.

That night, our massage therapist found that I was carrying the load of this friend and some of my psychic-development students in the form of upper-back discomfort. I truly cared about these people, but not to the point of hurting myself by carrying their pain. After the massage, I looked up the root of the word *care*, wondering if there was a common root between *care* and *carry*.

I found that the Latin root of *care* is "cura," which is also the Latin root word for *curative* or *cure*. That's the information I was seeking! Love wasn't about carrying another person; it was about caring. When we carry someone's pain, no one is helped. But when we simply care, we can cure them.

※ ※ ※ ※ ※ ※

Chapter 10

How to Attract
Everything You Desire

When I was a little girl, I told my father, "Someday I'm going to live right on the beach." We were visiting Newport Beach, California, at the time, and I'd fallen in love with the salt air, expansive horizon, seagulls, and ocean water. I never forgot that vow, and as a young adult who moved a lot, I frequently rented condominiums near rivers, lakes, and the ocean.

But my big dream was to have a house right on the beach. Steven knew of this dream, but our first step before we could manifest it was to believe that it was possible. At first I thought we'd have to compromise in order to afford our dream home.

"How about a house across the street from the beach?" I asked Steven. "One where we can still hear the waves, but where there might be another house in front of us."

"Why not go for exactly what we want?" was my husband's surprising reply. "If we truly believe we can buy a beach home, it will happen."

We had to eliminate all thoughts about *how* we'd afford such a place, and instead focus upon it being a reality. Everything I'd ever accomplished in the material world had occurred when I'd surrendered the hows and whys to Heaven's infinite wisdom. My only role was to hold the vision, feel it as a reality for which I already felt grateful, and then follow the Divine guidance I received.

Steven and I created a "Dream House Board." We found photographs of homes we liked in real-estate magazines and pasted them on a large piece of white construction paper. We also wrote phrases related to the dream such as: "Easily affordable" and "We closed escrow today!" on the board.

We hung our Dream House Board in our shared home office so that we'd see it frequently. Each morning we'd affirm together, "Thank you, Creator, for our beautiful oceanfront home that we love so much and easily afford." We spent time visualizing and feeling ourselves owning and living in the home, and we wrote detailed descriptions of those visions. These exercises strengthened our belief muscles, to give us the faith that the dream would come true.

The next step was to call a real-estate agent and look at oceanfront properties.

We had no idea what our price range for potential homes was, so we looked at all the beach houses for sale in Laguna Beach. Our agent, April Oswald, was an angelic young woman with a lot of patience and similar tastes in homes to our own. She took us to see many new places, but none of them were "it." By looking at homes that weren't right for us, Steven and I more clearly understood what we *did* want. Our friend and contractor Chris Prelitz went to see one house with us. He immediately showed us structural problems that would have cost a half a million dollars to correct, but neither Steven nor I felt disappointed. We hadn't liked it that much anyway.

* * *

After the home inspection, we went to Chris's house. Chris and his wife, Becky, work closely with Ron Roth, a Hay House author and former priest renowned for his spiritual healings. Ron had just returned from visiting Casa de Dom Inácio in Brazil, where he'd spent time with the healer John of God.

The Brazilian trip had powerfully shifted Ron. His eyes and aura were clearer and brighter than ever, exuding the powerful grace of a mystical high-priest. "Your aura looks like candle glow," I told him. "It's such a beautiful shade of pale yellow." The angels told me that Ron's claircognizance (his ability to receive messages directly from the Divine through thoughts and ideas) had opened up tremendously. He was a true channel!

Ron held my hand, and a powerful flow of loving energy pulsated straight to my heart. I was being exorcised of sarcasm and burnout from too many days spent traveling. I was so happy to receive this healing, as I wanted to enjoy the workshops I conducted on the road

He said, "I truly believe that what we're seeking on the deepest level is the Mother essence, that profoundly nourishing experience of the Divine. This is what Christianity has lost, this heart feeling. Sure, we can name the wonderful female saints from Mary Magdalene down through the ages to Hildegard of Bingen and Mother Teresa, all of whom I adore. But still, the question of the presence of the feminine principle goes far beyond the gender of any individual being. Authentic feminine essence is the balancing primordial energy that embraces and encourages us to live in a productive rather than reactive manner. It allows us to walk forward through doors that open into beauty instead of aggressively forcing our way through walls constructed out of fear and defensiveness.

"How different our traditions in the West are from those of India, where the ancient teachings of the feminine have never been suppressed into secondary status. The Hindu teachers have kept touch with Mother Kali and her balancing powers of fierceness and gentleness for dealing with our journeys through life and death. By stepping away from the strength of the feminine, our Western traditions also are shying away from direct experience with the most powerful and transformative forces of life. It's time that we recognize and bring back the feminine face of the Divine as essential to our innermost awakening."

Manifesting a Charmed Existence

Steven and I continued our daily affirmative prayers of "Thank you, Creator, for our beautiful oceanfront home that we love so much and easily afford." Our real-estate agent told us that there weren't any beach homes for sale with the criteria we'd come up with after looking at countless houses. Still, I felt a deep faith that the right place would come along at exactly the right time.

Besides, I was consumed with studying the *Urtext*. My focus was on the sections that discuss asking the Holy Spirit for what you want. The *Course* defines the Holy Spirit as the consciousness that can see both the pure spiritual truth as well as the human-made illusions. The Holy Spirit is the bridge that helps us switch channels from the ego-mind into our higher self, which is one with the Creator.

The *Urtext* says you needn't worry about asking the Holy Spirit for the "wrong" thing, or making poor decisions with your desires. That's because ego-driven desires are desires for nothing, which the Holy Spirit can't bring you. There's also a complete communication gap between the ego and the Holy Spirit.

We're not our egos, which are unreal illusions born of fear. So our true self can ask for whatever it desires. The Holy Spirit brings us everything, because the true self and its requests are real.

In other words, you can ask for joy, peace, and happiness, and the Holy Spirit brings these to you. In the illusion, these energies and emotions automatically attract and manifest happy life circumstances and experiences of prosperity, love, health, and everything else you want.

So first you ask for what's real, such as joy. This joy then attracts everything you could possibly desire within the illusion (such as a great relationship, wonderful health, great friends, and so forth).

Here are some real desires to request, and you can do so simply by thinking the thought, *Holy Spirit, I ask that you bring me:*

Peace	Grace
Happiness	Gratitude
Joy	Forgiveness
Stillness	Tranquility

Since you already own these characteristics, the Holy Spirit takes this request and flips a "happy switch" in your mind to reveal what you already have. A joyous person attracts the fun parts of life, supporting the old adage "The rich get richer." That's what it means to have a charmed life.

❊ ❊ ❊ ❊ ❊ ❊

Chapter 11

MOTHER MARY

My friend and Angel Therapy staff member Chris Marmes had purchased a crystal-healing bed from Kelly Willis. Chris, as you'll recall, sat in on my session with Kelly, and had been a comforting presence, so I felt really good about booking a session with Chris at her home. We chose the date of March 11, since 3 and 11 are powerful numbers—3 meaning "the ascended masters," and 11 meaning to "keep our thoughts locked upon desire instead of fear."

I climbed up on Chris's massage table, and she gently covered me with a soft blanket. I felt as if I were being tucked into bed by a magical goddess, and I relaxed.

She turned on the "triangulation" machine controlling the flickering colored lights behind the crystals. It reminded me of the sound of cards fastened to bicycle-wheel spokes with clothespins, as we did in childhood. That thought comforted me even more.

Her presence was so soft and gentle that I had no idea if Chris was in the room with me or not. My eyes were closed, and I was as relaxed as one could be without falling asleep.

Then I gasped and cried, "Mother Mary!" She stood before me holding a reddish-pink heart that was alive and glowing, and she mouthed the words, *"Help the children. You must help the children."* She didn't say how I was to do so.

The next words she said were, *"Go to Lourdes."* I gasped again. Lourdes was the famed healing well in France where a 14-year-old named Bernadette had visions of Mother Mary. Mary instructed the future saint to dig in the dirt near the grotto where her apparition appeared. Water soon filled the hole, and it eventually became a natural-springs well. Almost immediately, miraculous healings were reported by people who drank, or bathed in, the water. The springs became a sacred site that attracts thousands of visitors to this day.

Chris nodded knowingly when I told her about the vision and message from Mary after our session. She then added, "It was a fascinating session for me, too. I found attachments on your throat chakra from people wanting your voice, in the form of desiring a personal message from you, and there were also attachments on your solar plexus from people wanting your power. I worked with the angels to build a golden grid of protection around you, like golden filigree chain mail."

As I got in my car to drive home, I realized that my session had been so intoxicating that I wasn't alert enough to drive. So I sat and concentrated on the trees next to the car, paying particular attention to their gnarled roots going into the earth. The more I focused on the trees, the more grounded and "down to earth" I felt.

I thought of Steven's recent remark: "Is it possible to be too cleaned out, too pure, too sensitive? Perhaps we need some chemicals in our diet, some protection from harshness?"

Well, I was extra-sensitive since losing the 45 pounds and taking all chemicals out of my diet. I hadn't touched caffeine; sugar, alcohol, aspirin, chocolate, white flour—any chemicals or additives!—in ages. Was it wise to let go of all dietary armor in this world?

I recalled Chris's gift to me of the etheric golden chain mail. In ancient times, knights wore chain mail to protect themselves from physical weapons. In modern times, we weren't concerned with jousters riding toward us with swords. Instead, we needed protection from psychic weapons, such as stress, anger, jealousy, and violent media. So, donning a psychic suit of chain mail made perfect sense.

I drove home feeling very grounded and protected, anxious to tell Steven about Mother's Mary message and the fact that we were going to Lourdes.

Bernadette

"We're going *where?!*" Steven asked, astonished.

"Lourdes, in the south of France," I explained. "We're going to be in France anyway, right after our book tour in the U.K."

"Sorry, sweetheart, but not this year," he said. "This is our first trip to Paris, and we only have four days. We don't have time to go anywhere else in France."

"But Mother Mary was quite explicit," I said. "We *have* to go!" As usual, I wasn't concerned with the hows or whys behind my desire. I just knew I had to visit Lourdes.

I realized that Steven needed more information about Lourdes, so I purchased a DVD of the 1943 movie *The Song of Bernadette,* a touching account of Bernadette Soubirous's visions of Mother Mary.

We were both in tears by the end of the film, and Steven said, "Okay, I can see why you want to go to Lourdes. But can't we wait until next year when we can have more time there?" I remembered the urgency to Mother Mary's message and said, "I'm not completely sure why, but I have to go to Lourdes *this* year."

Steven nodded, still not convinced of the trip's feasibility. How would we see Paris and Lourdes in only four days, which included travel time to and from France?

The next day, Steven and I went to the Wild Oats Community Market to shop for food. "I'm going to the bank," he said. "Why don't you get started with shopping, and I'll meet you inside the store as soon as I'm done."

As I was selecting fresh organic produce, a woman in her 60s stopped me. I'd never seen her before.

She exclaimed, "You look so healthy!" I thanked her, and then she asked, "Do you know what I can do for fatigue?"

I blinked and thought about which vitamins to recommend. Then I realized I had to tell her the truth about calling upon angels to help with fatigue.

"What's your name?" I asked.

"It's Bernadette," she replied. This felt like an episode of *The Twilight Zone!* Surely, this was a sign from St. Bernadette and Mother Mary, to validate my need to visit Lourdes.

I asked Bernadette, "Have you ever heard of Archangel Michael?"

"No, I know nothing about angels," she replied.

"May I do an angel treatment for you?" I asked, oblivious to the fact that we were standing in a busy grocery store.

"Oh yes!" Bernadette exclaimed.

I saw large etheric cords extending from this woman's body. Etheric cords are energy attachments formed in fear-based relationships. When you have these cords, other people can drain energy from you, and they can also *send* negative energy to you.

So I said, "Archangel Michael, please cut any etheric cords that could be draining Bernadette's energy or vitality." She shuddered as Michael cut through her cords.

I then clairvoyantly looked into Bernadette's chest and saw obstructions. In my psychic-development courses, I'd found that nearly everyone could look inside another's person body by simply holding the intention to do so. Most people assume that they can't see inside of a body, so they never think to try it. But when they decide to look inside another person's body (especially for healing purposes), most find that it's a very natural and easy process.

I described the obstructions I saw in her chest. Bernadette nodded and explained that she had asthma and bronchitis, so I said, "Archangel Raphael, please come to Bernadette now and clear her lungs and passageways of any and all obstructions." I watched her breath deepen and the color of her face brighten from the nourishment given to her by additional oxygen and blood.

After our impromptu session, Bernadette thanked me profusely and inquired, "What do you do for a living?"

When I summarized my work as a teacher of the angels, Bernadette asked for my telephone number. "I need to see you again!"

"No," I replied, fully confident of the angels' guidance. "The angels will continue to help you now that you've invited them into your life. This work is about them, not me."

I hugged Bernadette and turned around to see Steven waiting and watching patiently. When he heard the woman's name, Steven's eyes widened. He's very sensitive to signs from the universe.

"Interesting," he said, "because I just spoke with Selvain, the French owner of Laguna Coffee Company, and he told me that Lourdes is a three-day trip minimum."

I felt the presence of the archangels and Mother Mary behind me. They knew that Steven was unsure about Lourdes, and they were helping by giving us both signs. I felt peace and joy, completely unconcerned with Steven's attitude toward the trip. I knew in my heart that somehow we'd be in Lourdes that year.

Besides, I was looking forward to the next day's trip to Kona, Hawaii, where we were teaching our Angel Therapy Practitioner (ATP) Course.

More Signs from Above

As I gazed at the ocean from our Hawaiian hotel room, I affirmed that Steven and I would own and live in a house with a similar view. I focused on my gut until it relaxed into the warm feeling that comes from full faith that an aspiration is going to manifest. I'd learned that this magical, warm sense of relaxation was an important key to manifesting. Whenever I could truly feel the reality of a dream in that area, the results were inevitable.

After the long flight to Hawaii, Steven and I were tired of sitting still; we wanted to exercise. So we decided to go to the gym to stretch and do a workout with weights, followed by an ocean swim.

When we checked into the spa, a young Hawaiian woman at the front desk greeted us. I gasped as I looked at her name tag. "Your name's Bernadette!" I exclaimed.

"Yes, it's a really unusual name, especially here in Hawaii, and especially for women my age," she commented.

As we walked to the weight room, Steven said, "Okay, that was more than just a coincidence. I'm still not sure how we're going to have enough time to go to Lourdes this year, but these signs are making me more open to the idea." I kissed my husband on the cheek, grateful that he was so attuned to universal energies.

After our workout, we walked to the ocean. I loved the feeling of jumping into the cool sea following a sweaty workout. I wore my snorkel mask to better see the colorful tropical fish and undersea plant life. I swam underwater like a mermaid, visiting my friends the fishes.

As the sun began to set, we moved toward the shore. "Look over there!" Steven called out. A sea turtle fed on seaweed near the shoreline. I waded up to the turtle and warmly said, "Hi, baby!" It felt like a reunion with a beloved friend.

The turtle swam directly toward me and stuck her head out of the water. I put my head down to her level, and she put her mouth directly on mine, in a very clear kiss! Her warm greeting made my heart pulsate with joy. She then swam up to me closer and put her front legs around my shoulders in a strong embrace. We were now hugging!

I lovingly stroked her chest, and the interaction was no different from the affection you'd share with a pet dog or cat.

After the turtle and I said good-bye to each other, Steven remarked, "It was clear to me that she deliberately sought you out for that kiss. When an animal acts unusually, it's a sign to heed. She, like all sea turtles, has 13 squares on her back. So she represents the goddess, especially the Earth Mother goddess, greeting and loving you."

"Yes," I agreed, walking arm in arm with Steven. "It's part of the return of Mary. Mary's name means 'the sea,' and also 'Mother.' With her return, we're balancing ourselves and reconnecting to Mother Earth, which includes respecting and honoring the Mother more, instead of the old, unbalanced male energy that disregarded the earth."

"I couldn't agree more," Steven said.

I felt so fortunate to have a husband who understood and honored the Divine feminine power and wisdom. Thank you, God! Thank you, Goddess!

Angel Therapy Training

It was now mid-March. I hadn't seen most of the Angel Therapy Practitioner staff since before the Harmonic Concordance of November 8 the previous year. That's when I'd received the instructions from Archangel Michael that led to my losing 45 pounds. So the staff was startled when they saw how much weight I'd lost. Naturally, they wanted to know how it had happened, yet one of the staff members, Gary Wiler (the amazing mediumship student in the Sedona class I wrote about in Chapter 1), had also dropped a tremendous amount of weight.

When I asked him about it, he said that he was on a diet similar to my own. However, Gary looked more than thin—he looked pale, gaunt, and fragile. I'd always liked Gary and wanted him to feel good, especially since the Angel Therapy Practitioner Course was going to be an intense week, even if we were in the paradise setting of Kona, Hawaii.

The class got off to a good start, with most of the participants choosing to go on an optional boat ride around the island to swim with wild dolphins. The friendly Hawaiian dolphins were wonderfully playful swimming companions for the class participants. The dolphins' magical Reiki-like energy also helped to clean and open the students' chakras, which made their angel readings during class time much better.

On the first morning of the ATP class, I paired the students, facing each other and holding hands. "Close your eyes and take some deep breaths," I gently instructed. "Now, imagine that you can see your partner's angels. What do you imagine that those angels look like?"

I gave the students a few moments to tune in to their partner's angels. By asking the students to "imagine" what the angels looked like, I gave them permission to see angels without worrying whether they were conjuring up the vision. After all, one reason why children easily see angels is because they don't worry whether it's make-believe or not. As we grow older and worry about such things, our spiritual sight dims.

"Hold the intention of asking your partner's angels the following questions," I instructed. "First, ask the angels, 'What would you like me to know about my partner?' Notice the answers you receive as feelings, thoughts, visions, or words.

"Next, please ask your partner's angels, 'What message would you like me to give to my partner from you?' Then notice the impressions that come to you."

I then asked the students to scan around their partner's head and shoulders, to notice other angels or departed loved ones. "Notice distinguishing characteristics in these beings," I said.

"Now comes the most important part of giving an angel reading," I added. "You've got to tell the person everything you saw, thought, felt, or heard concerning their angels and the messages. Tell your partner everything, even if you're unsure about it. Remember that the angels always speak with loving words and messages. Okay, go ahead and share with your partner now, and hold nothing back."

The students' expressions and mannerisms as they shared told me that they'd successfully connected with their partners' angels. Afterward, a few of the students shared remarkable stories with the class about their readings. The majority of students received accurate messages about their partners concerning topics that they couldn't have known about beforehand.

I told the class how our egos can block our psychic abilities. "You, like everyone, have an important life mission. Your inner Divine guidance will propel and support you every step of the way. The only thing that could block you is fear. For instance, if you strain or try too hard to hear the angels, you'll be blocked by the fear underlying the strain. That fear is, 'What if I can't hear my angels?' so you push to make it happen. Well, anytime you're afraid, you're in your ego. That's true for all of us, since everyone has an ego. The ego is 100 percent *not* psychic, and anytime we're in our egos, we'll be psychically blocked. On the other hand, your true self (the part of you that's naturally unafraid because it's one with God) is 100 percent psychic right now.

"The way to stay out of the ego is to focus upon service. When you're concentrating on helping another person, you won't worry about yourself, so you'll stay out of your ego. Always remember what the angels once told me: *'If you get nervous, focus on service.'*

"The ego will try to tell you that you're a fake, a phony, and not psychic. We call this the 'imposter phenomenon.' Basically, your ego wants you to stay afraid because it feeds on fear. The ego doesn't want you to remember or fulfill your purpose, because it wants you and other people to stay afraid. Yet, the ego is an unreal illusion, like a dark cloud trying to hide the light. I've found that the bigger someone's purpose is, the bigger their fear. If your soul agreed to help a lot of people, your ego is going to scream the loudest because it doesn't want you lifting fear from all those people. That's why I ask you to remember: 'If you get nervous, focus on service.' When your intentions are directed toward helping others, your ego's voice is dimmed."

On the fourth evening of the ATP Course, Steven led the students through a beachside ceremony. The students had channeled a message for themselves from Archangel Michael in answer to the question: "What do I need to release to be fully on my path and purpose?" They'd taken this written message and transferred its energy into an object of nature, such as a shell or a stone. (The transfer occurred at night while the student was sleeping, purely by setting the intention that this be done.)

The culmination of the releasement ceremony came when students held their objects of nature, meditated upon what they were releasing, then tossed the object into the ocean (we'd first asked the sea for permission, of course). This process was a powerful agent in releasing addictions, unhealthy habits, self-doubt, and toxic relationships.

Midway through the releasement ceremony, a white owl flew overhead. In Hawaii, white owls are called *pueo* or *aumakua* spirit guides who bring powerful messages. Their appearance also portends a death. The next day we discussed the owl sighting. Most students felt that the owl was a messenger from the spirit world, like an angel of death, letting us know of an imminent transition.

Goddess Power

One component of each Angel Therapy class is a goddess circle that I run for female students and staff members, while Steven simultaneously holds a men's gathering. Steven jokes that the men watch football, burp, and drink beer during these meetings, and I joke back that we women go shoe shopping. In truth, both genders receive a lot of validation during these brief, segregated meetings. There's something about being in a group composed solely of your own gender that frees you to speak your truth.

We women sat in a circle, and I explained the "Power Process" comprising the first half of our goddess meeting. I stood in the center and said, "This is Mike," holding up my wireless microphone. "Everyone say, 'Hi, Mike!' The group greeted the microphone with giggles.

"Mike is a tool for lightworkers to spread their messages and energies of love and light," I explained. "Many people are intimidated by Mike, but we need more lightworkers to feel comfortable with him. Lord knows that the people who work with lower energies are very comfortable using Mike to broadcast messages of fear over the radio and television waves." Everyone in the group nodded knowingly. "I'd like a few of you to push yourselves beyond your comfort zone, and learn how to get comfortable with Mike.

"We're going to do something called the Power Process. One of you will stand in the center of the circle holding Mike to amplify your voice. We want you to say something on the topic of power. It can be a story of how you gained your power back, why you're afraid of power, or a lesson for us all about power. You can say *anything*, as long as it's related to power.

"And here's the catch: We only want to hear from women who are normally shy and don't speak up in groups. Once you're finished speaking, please hand Mike to someone else in the audience who normally doesn't talk much. And please, ladies, don't psychically attack the person who hands Mike to you! Now, who wants to begin?"

After a long pause, the first woman stood up and said she'd been raised to believe that women should be pretty, but not much else. She'd gained personal power from life's trials, which gave her a choice to either die or grow stronger. We all applauded her courage, and she handed Mike to the next woman. We continued with the Power Process for an hour, with lots of tears, laughter, and applause. Everyone felt elated and inspired afterward.

It was time for us to begin the second half of our women's meeting: the Goddess Scarf Dance. We played music and danced, with each of us streaming a long, bright, and silky scarf behind us. Then I invoked goddesses, one by one, over the microphone so everyone could hear.

First I called upon Pele, the Hawaiian island goddess of passion and volcanos. Spontaneously, all the women danced faster like an indigenous tribe. They whooped and hollered as they caught Pele's fiery energy.

Next, I invited the presence of Brigit, the Celtic goddess of protection and healing. The group's dancing, chanting, and drumming rhythms shifted to match Brigit's more mysterious energy. I could almost see a mist enveloping the group, taking us back to ancient Ireland.

I then called the ocean goddess, Sedna, revered by Inuit tribes as the provider of summertime harvests and wintertime sustenance. Everyone in the group swayed fluidly with their scarves, like waves, mermaids, and dolphins.

After that, I called on Mother Mary. Many of the women became still, draped their scarves over their head, and swayed gently from side to side. I marveled at how synchronized our movements became in response to the unique energy of each goddess.

The final goddess I invoked was Quan Yin, the Buddhist bodhisattva of compassion, mercy, and forgiveness. "Ask Quan Yin to help you forgive yourself, and to have mercy and compassion for yourself," I suggested to the group. Many of the women put a hand to their heart, to anchor the healing occurring within us all.

Then we gathered back into a circle, standing side by side. At my suggestion, we each clasped one another's little pinky finger, to form a beautiful, strong chain of goddesses. We raised our clasped pinkies above our head and said in unison, "Goddesses, united forever."

A woman from the class said, "When women step into their power, it allows men to open their hearts." We all cheered upon hearing the truth of her statement.

※※※※※※

Chapter 12

THE OCEAN'S WOMB

To celebrate the completion of the ATP Course, the staff, Steven, and I chartered a boat so that we could swim in the ocean with dolphins. As our boat left Kona Harbor, a pod of these beautiful creatures excitedly jumped in front of us, delighting in their play.

The dolphins of Hawaii are the most animated and expressive I've experienced around the world. Perhaps it's their permanent smiling expression, their seemingly giggling laughter, the way they jump and spin into the air while swimming, or how they catch waves and bodysurf. Hawaiian dolphins are wonderful teachers who let us know the importance of playfulness.

As we passed by the dolphin pod and headed out into the ocean, I noticed a ring of white plumeria flowers scattered on the water. I felt that they were a memorial for someone who'd died.

We anchored in a bay and climbed from the boat into the warm ocean water. Soon, a large pod of playful dolphins swam toward us. I called to Angie Hartfield, a staff member who lives in Hawaii, to swim with me.

As Angie and I swam, the silent herd of dolphins quickly glided through the turquoise waters beside and below us. Angie and I swam along effortlessly at the same supersonic speed. Were the dolphins pulling us along an energy beam?

After an hour of swimming, we all climbed back onto the boat just in time to see a humpback whale and her baby swim by. Jeff, the boat's captain, had placed a special waterproof microphone in the water, specifically for the purpose of amplifying whale sounds. Sure enough, we heard the mother and baby singing the song unique to whales.

Clouds covered the sun, so it was time for us to head north where it was warm and clear. When I dove into the ocean at our new location, I was hypnotized by watching the strong sunbeams dance through the water.

The striped sun rays extended from the water's surface to the white sand below. I looked into the water with my snorkel mask, transfixed by bars of shimmering light surrounding me. I was in a light tunnel, like those described during near-death experiences. I felt the tunnel pulling me down toward the sand, yet it was an illusion, because I continued to float buoyantly on the surface. Then I realized that this dazzling light show in the clear turquoise water was clearing and opening my third eye!

Since I was unaware that I was drifting far from the boat, Lynnette came to get me. I asked her to look under the water with me, and we both became transfixed by the shimmering tunnel of white light. Someone else from the boat came to get us, and the same thing happened when we showed her the gorgeous sight. Finally, Captain Jeff snapped us all into awareness with his loud call.

As we swam to the boat, Lynnette and I compared notes about Gary, one of the few staff members who wasn't with us that day. I was very concerned that his energy and mood had been so low during the week. His hotel roommate had reported that Gary was behaving erratically and wouldn't listen to reason when he and Lynnette implored him to see a doctor.

Gary had finally admitted that he'd pretended his weight loss had been from dieting. He was actually terminally ill and had come to Hawaii to die after 16 years of struggling with his disease. He wanted to make his last days meaningful by spending them in selfless service during our angel course. He'd made the decision and was at peace with it. Gary had never discussed his illness with us because his family didn't know. Ashamed of his condition, he'd kept it a secret from everyone.

I thought back to the plumeria wreath we'd seen on the water that morning. "I felt like those flowers were a funeral memorial," I admitted to Lynnette, "and I tried to push out of my mind that they were a sign of Gary's death."

"Me, too," she said sadly while gazing at the ocean's horizon, where whales spouted water and breached with their tails pointed vertically in the air.

"So maybe the white owl the students saw *was* portending a death," I thought out loud. "Maybe the owl was an angel telling us about Gary."

Beginnings and Endings

After the boat trip, we all gathered at the home of Angie and her husband, Duke, to shower and change for the ceremony that was planned for that evening. Angie and Duke were renewing their wedding vows, and Steven and I were officiating as ministers. Steven and I had jointly married one other couple, and Steven had conducted many weddings on his own, yet this was our first marriage-renewal ceremony.

Everyone changed into dressy "aloha wear," and Angie presented us all with lei necklaces and palm-frond headpieces. I felt like a *Huna* (the term for Hawaiian shamanism) priestess by the time Angie had adorned me with flora.

Angie, Duke, their daughters, Steven, the staff members, some island friends, and I stood in a circle at a beachside park. The female members of our group stood on the ocean side of our circle, and the men stood on the mountain side, to signify the feminine and masculine energies of the ocean and mountains. Everyone took turns giving a blessing to Angie and Duke as the setting sun painted the clouds in bright colors.

Voices from another ceremony closer to the shoreline caught our attention. We all looked over to see the silhouette of a man holding an infant up to the setting sun, with a circle of people around him. "It's a baby christening!" Steven exclaimed.

"How beautiful that we're celebrating the renewal of Angie and Duke's marriage and a new birth simultaneously," I said.

So it was almost too perfectly synchronistic when we later discovered that Gary had died. During the wedding and christening, his death had also occurred, bringing the cycle of life full circle. Gary didn't want to return to the mainland. He wanted his last days on Earth to be on Hawaii amidst his spiritual family.

I thought of the Hindu goddess Kali, who's often feared and misunderstood. Many see Kali as a ferocious and powerful spirit who throws life-destroying temper tantrums. What Kali has taught me, though, is that she's not about revenge. She's about beginnings and endings, spring and summer, birth and death. Death isn't a punishment any more than birth is a reward. They're just cycles of life, which is what Kali oversees with great love and wisdom.

When we experience loss, it's natural to ask why. We want to understand the cause to prevent the situation from occurring again, but our conscious mind operates in three dimensions, with time and space restrictions built into the fabric of its logic. That's why our human mind can't understand the fourth-dimensional reality we actually live in, where space and time truly don't exist. The causes and reasons for beginnings and endings lie within the four dimensions, just out of reach of our logical minds.

Most likely you've had dreamtime soul-travel experiences where you attended school and were taught profound truths. Those teachings made perfect sense while you were dreaming, and you promised yourself you'd remember the knowledge upon awakening. But in the morning, you couldn't remember any of the teachings because they were based on limitlessness. The lessons get squished by time and space restriction beliefs we carry during our waking hours. Yet those dreamtime lessons are retained in our subconscious mind, where they're unconsciously helping us.

We may not be able to understand the Great Plan behind death, birth, and the cycles of life, but I believe that it's all in Divine Order, even if the underlying reasons are beyond our immediate comprehension.

I recalled the words of Manuel, the Mayan shaman who guided Steven and me through Chichén Itzá: "Mayans believe in duality," he'd said, "in positive and negative, death and birth." Manuel explained that death wasn't considered negative in the traditional Western sense of the meaning. "Negative" to Mayans meant endings, and "positive" meant beginnings.

Little did I know that I was in the cycle of a new beginning myself. . . .

❋ ❋ ❋ ❋ ❋ ❋

Chapter 13

MERPEOPLE

The next morning, Steven and I ate breakfast with Lisa and David Weiss, two of our Angel Therapy staff members. We'd enjoyed swimming with them in the ocean the day before, and Lisa had intrigued me with a comment she'd made about incarnated merpeople.

I'd written about mermaids who took on human form in my books *Healing with the Fairies, Earth Angels,* and *Angel Medicine,* yet I felt that there was much more I wanted to say. So, I'd created a formal survey and conducted interviews to find more information about merpeople.

Lisa, who sports long, flowing red hair; green eyes; and a genuine smile, told me that her interest in the topic started when she worked with marine animals during her college days: "I had recurring dreams about people being able to swim underwater without coming up for air," she said. "Then I had a lucid dream that I was digging in the dirt and found a shroud that reminded me of the Shroud of Turin, except the image was of a dolphin glowing with a neon-blue outline. I heard a high-pitched tone emit from the dolphin image, followed by thousands of nondescript voices that seemed to be downloading information to me.

"Then the dolphin in the shroud came alive, and it told me, 'We lived on land at one time. We were one with the humans.' The dolphin told me that his species was once humanlike when they'd walked on the earth. They shape-shifted and moved into the ocean after humans began misusing their power and abusing the environment. The dolphins believed that if they got away from humans and lived on their own in the ocean, they could wait until that time when humans became more peaceful and environmentally conscious. Then the dolphin looked at me and clearly said, 'Now it's time, so we're coming back to take over the world.'"

That was in 1988, a time when Lisa hadn't read any New Age books, had no knowledge of Atlantis, and her understanding of dolphins was very left-brained. So the dream frightened her, which led her to do metaphysical research. "Now I have a very positive outlook on the dream's meaning," Lisa explained, "and since that time, I've received so many signs that point to the return of the dolphins."

She tapped her left cheek and said, "This is one of the signs." There, on Lisa's cheek, was a perfect purple image of a jumping dolphin imbedded in her skin. It wasn't a birthmark or tattoo—this was like a "wine stain" in a very precise shape. "It appeared on my face immediately following my dolphin dream," she explained.

As part of her research, Lisa had a past-life regression. "When the hypnotherapist took me through a gate into my past life, I fell into water. The hypnotherapist asked me to look down at my feet and describe the type of shoes I was wearing. Well, I didn't have feet—I had dolphin fins!" Lisa tried two more regressions, with the same results.

Another time, a psychic who knew nothing of Lisa's dream or past-life reading told her, "You were a dolphin in your past life."

Later that day, Steven and I swam in Keauhou Bay, just south of Kona. As I frolicked with a pod of dolphins, I marveled at how similar their bodies were to those of humans, in both size and shape. I remembered Shannon Kennedy's report of the scientific study about the manatee being more similar to a human than a chimpanzee. Were dolphins our lost ancestors? I decided to do more research when we returned home.

As I looked at the dolphins, I saw geometric shapes like neon-colored scaffolding that forms triangles. These energy triangles surrounded each dolphin, and the shapes traveled with them as they swam. Most of the energy triangles were electric blue; but some were red, pink, or yellow.

I wondered if the triangular shapes were part of the energy complex of the dolphins' sonar system. Plato contended long ago that everything in the universe was composed of five basic geometric shapes, which are today known as "The Platonic Solids." All of these shapes are composed of triangles.

Were the pyramids erected in Atlantis, Egypt, and in Mayan and other civilizations in honor of these powerful shapes? Could the dolphins have connections to the pyramids? I definitely needed to study the links between dolphins, human origins, pyramids, and Atlantis.

That night while falling asleep, I saw an image of Gary in his new home in the spirit world. He beamed at me happily and said, "There's so much more here than you ever described!" He was in a pyramid of shimmering light, which was moving like rippling water. I thought of the grids of light with a pyramid appearance I'd seen around the dolphins that day.

As I did each night before sleeping, I visualized the entire planet being surrounded with white light for protection and healing. My energy felt too low to cover the earth that night, so I drew in power with deep breaths of clean Hawaiian air and saw my aura size expand as my power revitalized.

I then visualized covering the earth with a big, beautiful blanket of protective white light. Just then, Steven, on the brink of sleep, sat up and exclaimed, "Whoa! I just saw a big burst of white light!"

The Green Flash

The following evening, Steven and I sat on the beach to watch the sunset. We'd always hoped to see the famous "green flash" in which the setting sun momentarily shines a bright shade of green. Legend says that if you see the green flash, you'll be taken into the fairy realm. Well, we'd watched hundreds of sunsets over oceans, and had yet to see any color resembling green, so we didn't have much hope or expectation of seeing it. We mostly enjoyed the romance of sitting together as the sun set on another wonderful day in this Hawaiian paradise.

Then it happened! Just as the sun's half-circle ducked into the ocean, a huge flash of green light with lime-green points reflected back at us. Steven and I were almost knocked backward by the strong visual impact.

"The green flash!" we said simultaneously. It was a first for both of us.

A few minutes later, we got up and walked along an old trail through some volcanic rock near an ancient, sacred fishpond that natives had used in healing ceremonies. I felt as if I were in a heightened state of sensitivity, like the semi-trance between dreaming and awakening.

The trail was difficult to see as the sky darkened. Glowing lights moved above the trail, and as my eyes focused, I saw hundreds of ancient Hawaiian spirits. Someone had once told Steven and me about these deceased islanders called *ka huakai o ka po*, which means "night marchers" or "trail walkers." They were so clear that Steven, who normally doesn't see clairvoyantly, also saw them. The trail walkers walked wordlessly by us, yet there was nothing zombie-like or frightening about them.

At first I assumed that the trail walkers were earthbound spirits unaware of their death, but a voice told me that they'd chosen to stay close to the earth for environmental purposes. *"They're protecting the land,"* the voice assured me.

Before walking onto the sacred area, we twice asked the trail walkers for permission. Our second request caught the attention of an elderly, slightly shrunken and hunched-over medicine man. He walked on Steven's left side and accompanied him onto the sacred land. The medicine man spoke into Steven's left ear continuously as he led him. I dropped back behind to let the two men talk.

The medicine man accorded Steven tremendous respect, and I could tell that he recognized a fellow shaman. He told my husband, "You both haven't been ready to live on this island, but now you're being prepared. We [Hawaiians] have largely forgiven your ancestors for what they did to our people and land. But you, Steven and Doreen, must promise to help keep the land beautiful."

We then walked to a cave formed by a "lava tube," in which a large river of flowing lava had hardened like a giant hollow tunnel.

Steven took out the didgeridoo he'd been carrying, and after asking permission of the medicine man, he began playing music. There was a village of trail walkers in the cave as we arrived, partly because it was their longtime home, and partly because they knew of my husband's music-making. The nearly full moon had risen above the mountain tops, illuminating Steven and the trail walkers in a mystical light. I watched from a respectful distance, not quite prepared to go deep into the cave with them.

After Steven rejoined me, we walked with the medicine man toward the lake called Queen's Bath in Mauna Lani, north of Kona. This renowned healing bath was used by Polynesian women and Hawaiian royalty as a place for rejuvenation and healing.

Steven switched on the flashlight that he'd brought along. The medicine man frowned upon seeing it, and I caught his thought that it was rude and disruptive to our spirit friends, so Steven only switched it on when the dense trees blocked the moonlight and made it difficult to see where we were walking. As we veered from the path and into an old grove of trees that guarded Queen's Bath, we stepped on dead branches and leaves, and I was grateful that Steven was illuminating our footsteps.

Then the flashlight went out. "I don't understand," said Steven, fiddling with the switch. "I just put new batteries in this morning, and it's a brand-new flashlight." I looked at the medicine man. How powerful he was to break our flashlight! Yet I knew he'd help us on our journey without the need for modern lighting.

And he did. Queen's Bath was tucked behind a large and visible old fishpond near the Mauna Lani Resort. We first reached beautiful white sand marking the entrance to a small footbridge. While the energy of the lava-tube cave had been very masculine, Queen's Bath felt completely feminine, like a goddess retreat. Here, I saw many slim, beautiful Polynesian female trail walkers. Unlike the glowing but otherwise colorless trail walkers we'd met earlier (including our medicine-man guide), these women wore long, colorful gowns. The only way that I knew they were spirits was by their slow, reverent walking meditation, which was clearly from another era.

Steven and I joined their slow pace out of respect. The medicine man indicated that he'd wait for us at the footbridge, and Steven and I asked permission to enter. The ladies bid us both welcome with a bow and hand wave. Steven took off his shirt and shoes and entered Queen's Bath. "I was told to dunk myself in a purification ritual like a baptism," he explained.

I waded in up to my waist and said out loud, "I ask that any fears—or anything out of balance or out of sorts—be healed."

One of the women pantomimed for me to sprinkle water on Steven's head and on my own to seal the healing ritual. Spontaneously, Steven and I both exhaled deeply, indicating that we'd released something old and deep.

We'd both carried hibiscus flowers and kakui nuts with us to Queen's Bath, which we left as offerings of thanks. I silently asked the goddesses there to help Steven and me find a wonderful oceanfront home to buy.

The medicine man escorted us back to the main trail, and we headed toward our hotel. The path looked as busy as a New York city sidewalk, crowded with even more spirit walkers.

As Steven and I neared the hotel, a dark owl swooped down in front of us, startling us both. At that moment, we were alone on the trail, as the medicine man and all of the trail walkers had disappeared. The dark owl had swooped us back into ordinary reality, and we walked in a daze to our hotel. The hallways and lobby suddenly felt unreal and unnatural, and it took us some time to adjust back to "reality."

The next morning, I went to the beach before our flight back home. As I lay in the sun, I became annoyed by a woman talking loudly on a cell phone next to me. Then, a man on a riding lawn mower was loudly cutting grass next to the beach.

"I've got to get in the water!" I said aloud, grabbing my fins and snorkel mask. Once in the ocean, the noisy world disappeared, and I greeted my friends, the colorful tropical fish. Why couldn't I just stay here with them?

I could only hear my breath through the snorkel, which reminded me of a song by the band Angel Earth called "Find That Place." The lyrics are: "When I stop and hear my breathing, I can hear my inner voice."

I felt so peaceful that my ego couldn't stand it anymore, so it screamed at me: "Why can't you be at peace with human noise?!" The ego momentarily made me feel guilty and ashamed as I heard its question.

Fortunately, I was more practiced at noticing the ego's cunning digressions from peacefulness. My higher self quietly told me, "*The noise you had difficulty with came from technology and machinery, not from the individuals involved. You were irritated by the intrusion that mechanics played on your peaceful and restful morning, that's all. Forgive yourself, forgive the nature of the mechanical beast, and forgive all of the people involved. Then move on."*

Parental Gifts . . . and Guilt

As much as I loved Hawaii, it was always so good to return home and sleep in my own bed. It had been a good trip, and a wonderfully smooth flight home. As I fell asleep that night saying my prayers of gratitude, a voice told me that my mother's prayers for me were a big reason for my worldly success. The next day I called to thank her, and she was her usual humble self.

The following evening, the screeching siren of an emergency vehicle woke me up, and I immediately worried about my son Charles. I turned the worry into action by surrounding him with protective white light and invoking extra guardian angels.

I climbed out of bed, walked to the bathroom, and caught a glimpse of my tense expression in the mirror. *I'm so tired of worrying about my children!* I thought. *It's so draining and such a drag. I've been worrying about them since my pregnancy with Charles more than 25 years ago. That's way too long to carry the burden of worry.*

I thought of the message I'd received the prior evening about my mother's prayers. How fortunate I was that she didn't worry, but instead visualized positive things for me. She truly focused on desires and not on fears. I vowed to do the same for my children and for myself, and asked my angels for help in doing so.

That night I slept more soundly than I had in some time, having completely surrendered my parental-worry habit to the angels.

✹ ✹ ✹ ✹ ✹ ✹

Chapter 14

THE PRIESTESS PARTY

It was mid-April, so some girlfriends and I hired a limousine to take us to Los Angeles to celebrate my birthday, along with the birthdays of two other friends, Shannon Kennedy (the Ayurvedic doctor I spoke of earlier) and Shien-Linn, a beautiful physician's assistant. I would be in England on my birthday (April 29), so we were celebrating mine, as well as Shannon's March birthday and Shien-Linn's—she was also born in late April. We each wore a sparkly scarf that made us feel very goddess-like.

Our destination: Juliano's Raw restaurant. Juliano is a celebrated raw-food chef and author of *Raw: The Uncook Book*. Raw food mimics traditional meals but uses only uncooked vegetables, nuts, and fruits in ingenious ways. The menu at Juliano's restaurant includes tacos, sushi, pizza, hamburgers, and the like—all completely meatless and dairy free—and all completely delicious.

I'd eaten at Juliano's San Francisco Bay–area restaurant before he'd moved to Los Angeles. My former routine was to eat dinner at Juliano's and then head to the Palo Alto Unity Church to give angel readings. My readings were extra-clear and detailed whenever I'd conduct them with a belly full of raw food.

Raw fruits and vegetables deliver nature's life force with each bite. Cooked, canned, and frozen foods don't have much life force, as life can't survive in an oven, can, or freezer, so my girlfriends and I were excited about getting naturally high from the raw food at Juliano's.

Inside the limousine, we exchanged birthday gifts. Judith Lukomski gave me a large piece of aventurine crystal, the stone I was told to work with in my dream. Her gift came in a beautiful luminescent pouch with a drawstring, which I slipped onto my belt. "That's how people carried their crystals in ancient times!" Judith laughingly remarked.

I felt the energy of the aventurine immediately surge upward to my chest. Judith explained that aventurine is a wonderful crystal to open and clear the heart (physically and emotionally). "I guess this means that I'm supposed to be even more sensitive and feel emotions even deeper," I joked. "Okay, I want a guarantee that I won't get hurt if I allow myself to feel more!"

Chris Marmes (my friend with the crystal-healing bed) quipped back, "Don't we all?!"

I gave Shien-Linn a crystal wand as her birthday gift. Shien-Linn is a tall, thin young woman with long, silky dark hair and a beautiful face, smile, and soul. She was new to metaphysics, and we'd all taken her under our wing.

"Every priestess needs a crystal wand," I said as I handed it to her in a white velvet pouch. She pulled out the extremely feminine pink-and-white wand, embellished with both clear and rose quartz crystals. We then gave Shien-Linn rudimentary lessons on working with a wand.

On the way home from Juliano's, the Los Angeles freeway was congested with traffic, so we all encouraged Shien-Linn to use the magic wand. Tentatively, she pointed it at the traffic and asked it to move. "Command it, Shien-Linn!" we instructed. "Use the full force of your power and convictions!"

Lynnette said, "Take a deep breath, go inside yourself, and connect with your heart. See or feel what you truly desire to manifest. Then call upon the angels, Divine goddesses, and ascended masters to assist you. Put that intention with your out-breath into your wand. Next, with one great swish of your wand, say, 'It is so!'"

Judith said, "Sorceress, are you prepared to make wishes come true? Do you feel the wand's legacy of magic, power, healing, and grace vibrating within its stones' beauty? Its energy reflects the Divine love and universal wisdom found within you. This exquisite light is amplified and directed by the physical presence of crystal friends. Just as with human loved ones, each mineral is a unique treasure willing to share your journey. Still, you're responsible for the design of your experiences. Your prayers, intention, and focus activate the infinite possibilities of life. My wish for you is to live your life in joy discovering the brilliant crystalline energy within you."

Then Shannon said, "Matter is energy. Put your energy into a pinpoint of intention, and allow it to manifest. Energy is will in action."

Chris said, "Shien-Linn, beautiful goddess, know that this gift is about remembering the magic and reclaiming your power. Believe it is possible, know it is done, and as you believe, so it is."

We were like the fairy godmother in the Disney version of Cinderella, giving Shien-Linn our *Bibbidi-bobbidi-boo!* lessons in spell-casting.

Shien-Linn moved her body to gather strength and power, and her face became serene and confident. She pointed her wand to the traffic and said, "Move! Now!" There was no anger in her voice, just authoritative power. The whole energy within the car buzzed with a palpable presence and velvety energy.

The limousine driver had heard all of this, and said he was willing to try anything to escape the gridlock. So when the traffic parted within seconds of Shien-Linn's command, we all cheered, including our driver.

＊＊＊＊＊＊

Chapter 15

Meeting the Dalai Lama

When I'd read aloud my intention to meet the Dalai Lama to my friends during our New Year's Eve ceremony, I felt in my gut that it would happen. So I was thrilled to learn that he was appearing at the University of California, Irvine, campus near my home. I immediately purchased tickets to the event.

I researched the protocol for meeting the Dalai Lama and discovered that it was traditional to present him with a special white silk scarf called a *kata*. I purchased two katas through an online Buddhist-supplies store, one for myself and one for Steven.

At first I tried to arrange a private meeting with His Holiness. I contacted his office to interview him for this book, and the Hay House publicity team did the same. We were told that His Holiness was definitely not giving interviews on this tour—yet I *knew* I was going to meet him. I had no choice but to turn the whole thing over to Heaven and trust that it would somehow happen.

The afternoon of the Dalai Lama's talk, I put on a pretty but conservative dress and placed the katas in my purse. I had no doubt that I'd meet him that day, and saw myself presenting the kata to His Holiness.

As we drove to the Bren Events Center at the university, I was amazed by the crowds jamming to get into the building. Security guards lined the streets and checked each person. Cell phones weren't allowed inside and had to be left at a special security stand outside, where you were given a claim ticket to retrieve your phone after the event. Since virtually every person in Southern California is plugged in to technology, the cell-phone security line was long and slow-moving. Fortunately, Steven and I hadn't brought our phones, so we sailed through the metal detectors and into the arena.

A hush settled over the audience as the Dalai Lama entered and sat in a beautifully carved chair center stage. I noticed his beautiful violet and emerald green aura, mixed with some yellow. These colors showed his spiritual gifts of healing and a clear connection that enabled him to receive messages from the Divine. The yellow indicated some stress connected to his mission, which required him to travel ceaselessly as a spokesperson for Buddhism, as well as Tibetan freedom.

The Dalai Lama's easygoing countenance showed his devotion to meditation. He appeared to be someone who didn't think much about materiality, as all of his needs were met. I could tell that he lectured because of an inner calling, coupled with his sense of loving duty. The Dalai Lama's English was charmingly stilted, so an interpreter translated his words for the talk.

"Inner strength mixed with the right attitude equals a meaningful and happy life," His Holiness began. "If you have anger in your heart, it's impossible to create an affectionate atmosphere." He explained that drama pushes away love within relationships.

"A compassionate attitude really brings a positive atmosphere, which allows the elements of the body to work properly. Then there's no need for sleeping pills or tranquilizers." The Dalai Lama explained that the more strongly we feel compassion, the more effectively this emotion helps us.

"Self-awareness is the key to noticing your emotions. Anger and jealousy objectify their target," he added, explaining that when we feel these negative emotions, the person toward whom they're directed ceases to be humanlike to us. "When we're angry or jealous, our focus narrows, and we ignore other factors involved in the situation. To heal this, we need to use a holistic viewpoint, instead of the narrow focus of blame.

"Negative emotions arise primarily out of habit," the Tibetan leader told the transfixed audience. "Once you have the strong conviction of the consequences of negative emotions, you would no longer be willing to embrace them, and you would be more likely to choose and develop positive emotions. Once you have this basic outlook on these emotions, whatever actions you take based upon positive emotions is what we call 'ethical.'"

The Meeting and the Blessing

As the presentation ended and everyone stood to give the Dalai Lama their enthusiastic ovation, I told Steven, "Okay, time to go meet him. Are you coming with me?"

"It's not happening," he replied. "There are too many people here."

"Okay," I said, stepping over Steven's legs so I could walk down the aisle toward the stage where His Holiness was exiting.

I opened my kata scarf and walked in a direction intersecting with him as he walked offstage. I held up the kata to the security guard and said, "I'd like to give this to His Holiness," and the guard moved aside to let me through.

I held up my kata so that the Dalai Lama could see it, and he walked straight toward me! I handed him my offering, and he held it with his eyes closed, sending blessings into the white silk fabric. Then he put his face very close to mine so our foreheads nearly touched, and he looked me straight in the eyes. His eyes were smiling, and he was fully present and so lively. He had a huge, happy grin on his face.

The intensity of the moment was almost unbearable. The Dalai Lama's energy and personality was unlike anyone I'd ever met: He was so pure, so childlike, yet so regal! It was unworldly, really.

In my mind, I sent him the thought, *I love you. God bless you for all you do and for who you are!* I felt so much gratitude for his tireless service to the world and to the cause of peace, and I received the strong message that I needed to meditate more often.

Then, other people from the audience who saw me having a private moment with His Holiness gathered and pushed behind me. The Dalai Lama put the kata scarf around my neck, as his gift to me after filling it with blessings. Then his security guards whisked him away. He was gone.

I was shaking. Joannie Light, an Angel Therapy Practitioner and staff member, had witnessed the entire interaction, and she came over to revel in the moment with me. As we hugged, I found myself speechless. Fortunately, Joannie is so psychic that we didn't need to exchange words. She told me her own miracle story of how she'd just purchased her third-row-center seat the prior evening, even though the event had been sold out for weeks.

Joannie and I found Steven in the crowd, and I hugged him with excitement. When he didn't warmly embrace me, I looked into his eyes and saw that he was hurt and angry that I'd met the Dalai Lama without him.

I empathized with Steven's pain, even if it seemed illogical to me—after all, I'd asked him to come with me! As we walked to our car, Steven said, "You're ballsier than I am." It sounded like a put-down.

I stopped and looked at him and replied, "Yes, you're right. I *am* ballsy. This is who I am. It's one of the reasons why I'm successful, because I have no fear of following my visions."

Steven's angry gaze continued. "It reminds me of my mother, who was also ballsy, and she used to embarrass me." Then he added, "But you didn't embarrass me today."

"Well, you're projecting your mother issues onto me," I retorted.

"And you project your father issues onto me, so we're even!" Steven said, finally smiling.

But I wasn't done. "I can't and won't hold back from following my guidance," I said. "I'm frequently right, and you should follow my lead, whether I'm a woman or not."

"I do," he concurred. "Like when you said we needed to go to Lourdes, I finally agreed. In fact, when you first mentioned traveling there, I knew deep down that we were going. I just needed to fuss a bit at first."

We hugged and went out to dinner, where the creamy peanut sauce on our Thai food soothed our strong emotions. Steven and I could never stay angry with each other.

The next morning, Steven apologized first thing. "I'm sorry I was such a butt," he said. He went on to explain that he was facing his own shyness and sense of inadequacy. The situation had been a painful opportunity for him to look at his self-limiting beliefs. I thanked him and gave him a big hug and kiss.

An hour later, an audio-recording-company producer sent us an e-mail saying: "We want to interview you for our audio series called 'Standing on the Shoulders of Spiritual Giants.'" At first, Steven assumed they wanted to interview me. It took him a minute to realize that *he* was the spiritual giant the company wanted to interview.

My being powerful had inspired my husband. It was similar to something I'd told him when we were first dating and he'd had some trouble with my power. I'd said, "Look, I'm not going to shrink my aura to suit you, so you'd better increase yours if you can't handle my being this powerful. *Make* yourself more powerful!" And he had.

So many times while teaching lightworkers in my Angel Therapy courses, I'd have similar discussions with my students. I'd reassure them that power wasn't synonymous with being aggressive or competitive. That belief comes from the fear that you have to grab your share before anyone else does. Power is about knowing clearly what you desire, without worrying about "how" it will manifest. It comes from following your inner visions and guidance without delay.

Feminine power means being receptive to all the gifts life constantly offers. After all, feminine energy is receptive. Women become unbalanced when they only give and don't allow themselves to receive. Many of my female students complain that their prayers go unanswered; however, this is because they're unwilling to receive Heaven's gifts, which come through various sources. One such source is when people offer to help you. You'd be surprised by how many people push away offers of help!

Sourcer-esses must dance in their feminine energy and be gracious receivers of life's generous offerings. Say *yes* to offers of help, and *thank you* to gifts, and watch your life begin to take magical turns!

In meditation, I received the following message: *"Lightworkers are becoming stronger and also more sensitive. You're becoming more sensitive to your own natural rhythms, healthy options, and inner guidance. You're becoming strong enough to take steps to keep a healthy lifestyle and also follow your inner guidance. It's important to balance strength and sensitivity. If you're strong without being sensitive, that's when power can be too aggressive. When you're sensitive without being strong, you won't have the confidence to put your guidance into action."*

✳ 🖼 ✳

The next day as Steven and I were packing our bags to leave for London, April, our real-estate agent, called to say that a Laguna Beach oceanfront home had just been listed in our price range. *Could we come and see it?* she asked. *No, we were leaving for the airport in a few hours.*

We decided that if the home was meant for us, it would still be for sale when we returned home in one month. The home sold one week later while we were still in London. Obviously, it wasn't meant to be.

※※※※※※

Chapter 16

THE ISLE OF AVALON

Steven and I arranged for a holiday midway through our United Kingdom book tour. It was my birthday, and I wanted to spend it in Glastonbury, one of my very favorite locations on Earth.

On our first evening, Steven and I attended a drumming-and-chanting circle facilitated by an author named Jana Runnalls. As we entered the room, someone handed me a Remo vegan drum. (The Remo company makes drums without leather or other animal products.) I marveled at how the Universe provided, as Remo was the brand of drum I owned at home in California.

We sat in a circle, beating our drums in unison while Jana called in the seven directions: east, west, north, south, earth, sky, and within. Then Jana said, "Let's do a drum-and-chant journey in honor of Beltaine, starting with the sacred marriage."

The ancient Celtic holiday of Beltaine is held near May 1 of each year, to celebrate springtime and to appeal to fertility goddesses for bountiful crops. It's traditional for romantic partners to "jump the fire" on Beltaine, clasping hands as they leap over a bonfire together. Doing so signifies that the relationship will last at least until the following Beltaine.

The "sacred marriage" Jana spoke of is the merging of the male and female energies within us all. Sometimes, as in relationships, our inner man and woman bicker, ignore, or misunderstand each other. In the mystical marriage, they unite and cooperate. (More recently, the term has also come to mean a nun or female saint's devotion to Jesus.)

For our Beltaine ceremony, we chanted about the male energy of fire and the female energy of water. We also chanted about the sacred marriage of the god and goddess, and of fire and water coming together.

The Elements

The next morning, I thought about the previous evening's chants and invocations to the elements. The elements were such a foundation to Celtic spirituality, and I decided to go to the healing Chalice Well and meditate on it.

As I sat by the well, deep in meditation about water and fire and their practical applications, I heard:

"Water is the nurturing mother that washes away impurities. Fire is the powerful father that burns away impurities." I asked whether the elements of air and earth could purify us, too.

"Fire has been used in Imbolc [the February 1 Celtic fertility celebration] *to burn away old refuges of previous crops to make way for new crops. It purifies by removing the dross and the old. It is instant.*

"Water, like a mother, is more gentle in loosening the old from its roots, so it can wash away rather than being completely destroyed, as with fire."

I asked whether air purifies. *"Air oxygenates and works together to make fire burn more brightly. It's also a component of water."*

Then I asked about earth. Did it purify? *"Earth absorbs toxins out of the air, water, and the residue of fire, and she transmutes these toxins with her deep love.*

"All four elements work perfectly together. They must be balanced in proper precision to be the most useful (which is your word, Doreen) in practical terms. Just as the male and female must both be addressed, loved, and healed, so must you learn to live in harmony with all the elements.

"You can do this by visiting and living in a variety of locales: Mountains afford the opportunity to connect with earth and air; beaches, lakes, and rivers allow you to connect with water; and desert landscapes put you in touch with fire.

"Use all four elements to purify yourself, first in thought, then in deed, then in physicality. Calling upon the goddesses and angels of the

elements simplifies this process for you, as they're already aligned with a particular element. Just be sure to keep it in balance, and don't just work with fire elementals, for instance, without also working with associates of the other elements. If you only work with fiery Brigit, for example, your life will become imbalanced. There's a strong need to invoke, and work with, equal numbers of deities of water [like Aphrodite, Sedna, or Yemanya], *air* [such as Arianrhod or Nut], *earth* [Demeter or Persephone], *and fire* [Brigit, Pele, or Vesta]."

Then I asked why so many healings are associated with sacred wells and pools. The answer was: "*Water is the easiest of the four elements to consume. Don't forget that water is also high in mineral content, which is earth. It also contains oxygen, which is air. The nurturing feminine qualities of water (especially gently running water) make it easier for people to open their hearts, trust, and make themselves vulnerable as they drink of or bathe in it.*

"*Faith is a huge part of the healing equation. The prayers and faith imbued into the waters are powerful, as you will especially discover in Lourdes. Water is associated with bathing, which aligns it closely with cleansing and purification. So much of health and healing comes from the casting off of guilt, and water allows us the physical opportunity to bare and cleanse away guilt through ceremony—to wash away the past, if you will.*

"*The ocean water is intimately connected to the moon cycles, and therefore to the feminine cycles and energies. Oceans show the power of the moon.*"

That night in a dream, I was shown that our crown chakra is the brightest, like the Northern Star. In the dream, I was told that this is often misunderstood, and we try to make all of the chakras the same size and brightness. Since the crown chakra is the God/Goddess chakra, it is necessarily the brightest.

The Goddess Temple of Glastonbury

With its centuries-old architecture and the medieval dress that people wear while walking down the street, Glastonbury harkens back to ancient Celtic times. It's an oasis for spiritual seekers to find peace, quiet, and quaint book and crystal shops.

Visiting Glastonbury.

I'd heard about the Goddess Temple in Glastonbury and had made a point to meet with its founder, Kathy Jones, the author of *The Ancient British Goddess*. We met at the temple an hour prior to the Beltaine Eve ceremony that would be held there that night.

We began talking about my work with the angels, and Kathy said, "The swan is the power animal of the Celtic goddess, Brigit. I believe that swans shape-shift into angels, and vice versa." To Kathy, Brigit is very connected with the angels.

Kathy said that she'd had a longtime dream of creating a goddess conference. "I'd been holding one-day ceremonies, but then the goddesses gave me the idea to continue them over the course of several days." Still, the idea of organizing a conference was overwhelming for her.

So, Kathy went for a walking meditation on the Glastonbury Tor, a 500-foot-high hill with a winding labyrinth pathway leading to its peak. As she walked along, she prayed, "Goddess, transform me as you will." One week later, Kathy intuitively knew that she'd hold the conference the following year. A close girlfriend offered to help.

Two weeks after making the commitment and setting the conference into motion, Kathy was diagnosed with cancer, and she began radiation and chemotherapy. She endured nine months of treatment while organizing the conference. She recalls sitting in bed with no hair, feeling wretchedly ill, while still typing envelopes.

In retrospect, Kathy now realizes that the project gave meaning to her life and helped her endure her cancer. Her health improved, the conference was successful right away, and it's now an annual sold-out event.

Kathy also runs the busy Glastonbury Goddess Temple, located on the second floor of a plaza surrounded by a public library and a crystal store. She opened the temple after visiting sacred sites dedicated to goddesses. "They were all in ruins!" Kathy recalled. "So I decided that I had to open a goddess temple where we could conduct ceremonies all year long."

We talked about the ancient romantic history of Glastonbury, and its existence as an island called Avalon. "Avalon is still here," Kathy said. "Glastonbury is the outer world you experience with your physical senses, while Avalon is the inner world. To me, it's about opening the heart and surrendering to the Goddess and her love. So many women have no idea who the Goddess is! To me, she's the source of all things. She's the void, love, and wisdom incarnate. She's everything."

I asked Kathy about balancing the male and female energies, and she replied, "Sometimes I see the Goddess in balance with God as her partner, and it's usually a projection of how I'm feeling at that moment. This is especially true at Beltaine, as it's one of the few times that we allow men to peek into the Goddess because of the fertility rituals."

Our conversation ended when it was time to prepare for the Beltaine Eve ceremony. Kathy had suggested that participants dress in red in honor of the fire element, so I wore a floor-length maroon velvet goddess gown with bell sleeves and a ribbon lace-up bodice. Most women and men attending the event also dressed in red velvet.

Everyone sat on bright silk pillows lining the temple's lavender walls and purple carpeting. The temple was lavishly decorated for Beltaine Eve with seven-foot wicker female figures wearing flowing scarves and red sarongs.

The Goddess Temple in Glastonbury at Beltaine, with the Maypole in the foreground and the wicker goddesses in the background.

In the center of the room, brightly colored ribbons hung from a ceiling-high maypole. Traditional symbols of the male and female union associated with May Day and spring, maypoles are six-feet-or-taller poles draped in long colored ribbons. Men and women hold the ribbons and dance in opposite directions so that the ribbons are woven together around the pole.

Three stick ponies leaned against one wall, symbolic of the white horse that the Welsh moon goddess Rhiannon rides between the spiritual and material worlds. An altar draped in red velvet sat below a large painting of Rhiannon—depicted with long hair, bare breasts, and a red skirt—coming out of the sea like Aphrodite with a maypole and the Tor behind her. The flickering light of pink-and-white candles gave the painting and temple a soft glow.

The Beltaine Eve ceremony began with a procession of six women dressed in long red-velvet gowns, each wearing flower wreaths on their heads. With their charming British accents, each woman read an invocation to the goddesses of the four directions. Then we stood and faced the maypole in the center of the room as they called upon The Lady of Avalon and Morgan Le Fey, to whom the temple was dedicated. I softly cried at the thought of how goddesses had been pushed out of spirituality and religion until now.

A temple woman invoked the goddesses of love to symbolize the mystical marriage and fertility rituals of Beltaine Eve. As she called upon Aphrodite, Freyja, Bast, and Sarasvati, she held up a bowl of strawberries and said, "Whomever would declare their love to a person, partner, or friend can have a strawberry to share with that other person, who isn't allowed to touch the strawberry. It just has to be passed between the two persons' mouths."

A few couples, including Kathy Jones and her husband, participated in this fun strawberry ritual. Then Steven raised his hand and loudly said, "I hereby proclaim my love for Doreen!" He put a strawberry in his mouth, bit into it, and then kissed me with half the strawberry going into my mouth. The participants applauded us, as they had for the other couples.

People began circling the maypole, and each person grabbed the end of a ribbon hanging from the top of it. The men walked clockwise with their ribbons, while the women stepped counterclockwise around the pole. The result was a beautiful dance of people walking and ducking elegantly, while weaving the ribbons together.

Three women "rode" the stick ponies, and I thought, *That looks like so much fun!* Kathy walked over to me and asked if I wanted to ride the white stick pony. Of course I did, but I hesitated out of embarrassment of the thought of doing so in front of a roomful of adults. So I said to Steven, "Why don't you ride it?" He replied, "It's for Rhiannon—a man can't ride it!"

Kathy asked me again, and this time I summoned the courage to say, "Yes, I'd love to!"

I rode around the maypole and was given a dark blue ribbon to participate in the weaving and dancing while riding atop my white stick pony. Far from feeling foolish, I felt elated, and deeply connected to ancient days of ceremony and celebration.

Then it was time to go outside and jump the Beltaine flame. In the courtyard, a brass cauldron with hot coals was on fire. We all gathered outside, and one by one, couples jumped the flame. Steven took my hand, and I gathered my long hem in my other hand so it wouldn't catch on fire. We jumped over the cauldron together, signifying our commitment to one more year together.

After the couples jumped, individuals had the option of jumping solo over the flame to signify their intentions for the coming year. Steven decided to jump the flame to anchor his personal intentions. I also wanted to jump solo, but once again felt self-conscious. Why, when I spoke in front of thousands of people annually, was I self-conscious in front of these relatively few individuals?

Being a Source-eress requires you to be aware of your fears and then face them. A Source-eress must walk through her fears as a way of overcoming them, as I had while scuba diving in Australia. So I mustered up my courage, held my dress hem, set my clear intentions, and jumped. Like most fears, in retrospect I wondered why I'd ever felt nervous.

After the ceremony, we ate at the Galatia Café on High Street near the temple. A woman who looked and sounded just like Joan Baez sang, well, Joan Baez songs. Glastonbury is like traveling back not only to Arthurian times, but also to the 1960s! Steven and I didn't stay long to listen to her songs after we'd finished our meal, though. After all, the next morning was Beltaine, and we were planning on attending the sunrise ceremonies. So we walked home to our bed-and-breakfast to get some rest before our early morning.

As I undressed, I thought about how I'd enjoyed wearing my red gown on Beltaine Eve. Although I'd been frequently told that red was a flattering color for me, I rarely wore it. I'd always assumed it was because I didn't like calling attention to myself. But that couldn't be, since I frequently wore bright purple.

I was afraid of what red symbolized: fire, conflict, loud noise, and strong energy. *I need to bring more fire into my life,* I thought. *Not the conflict aspect of fire, but the positive side, especially as it pertains to personal power.*

I remembered how a few days earlier, I'd been accosted by references to fire! In the morning while exercising at our London hotel gym, the television blared out reports of brush fires blazing in Southern California. An hour later, our hotel ran a very loud fire-alarm test. That afternoon, we drove to the city of Bristol, where the medium Gordon Smith and I would give an evening seminar.

As we checked into our Bristol hotel, the clerk insisted that Steven and I read the hotel's fire-safety procedures while she stood by. At lunch, Gordon said that the clerk had done the same thing to him. I'd stayed in hotels worldwide and had never once been instructed, or even mildly urged, to read the fire-safety manual!

Right before that evening's Bristol seminar, I sat in my dressing room meditating. The first thing I saw when I opened my eyes was a large sign reading, IN CASE OF FIRE . . .

That's when I recognized the pattern of fire-related signs within the same day. At first I worried that it was an omen of a tragic fire.

Then I realized that it was about purification. I asked my angels to teach me what the fire symbols meant.

That night I received my answer. Much like the angels of Chalice Well had told me, the elements needed balancing. The water within my body, soul, and psyche needed to be balanced with fire and the other elements. Perhaps *that's* why my body had retained water all those years!

The Beltaine Sun Rising Over Avalon

When the alarm clock rang at 3:30 the next morning, Steven and I climbed out of bed without complaint or protest. I slipped into a long purple-velvet gown and overcoat, with warm purple-chenille gloves and flat black walking boots. Steven wore a white poet's shirt, black slacks and shoes, a large cinch belt, and a purple-flannel cape. We knew that most participants would be dressed similarly, as the Beltaine ceremony flyers suggested ceremonial wear. In fact, the local Pixie

Archangel Michael's Tower atop the Glastonbury Tor.

Tailor clothing store had nearly run out of goddess gowns and poets' shirts because pre-Beltaine sales were so high.

As Steven and I walked to the Tor, the sky was velvety black, the town was eerily quiet, and a misty fog hugged the ground. I also had the distinct feeling that we were being followed. "Brigit and Archangel Michael, protect us!" I said, and uttered continuous affirmations until I felt safe and calm.

We walked up the foot of the Tor, surprised that no one else was around. Where were the Druids who supposedly spent each Beltaine night at Archangel Michael's Tower at the top of the Tor?

Then we saw the figure of a man in dark clothing standing in front of us on the path. My heart thumped as we walked toward him. As we progressed through the mist, I noticed that he was quite large. *Thump, thump.*

I hesitated as we approached him. Who or what was this man? Was he spirit or solid? A Druid looking for someone to sacrifice to the sun god Bel?

We nodded and grunted a hello to him as we passed by. He just stood there smoking a cigarette and looking at us. As we went past him, his footsteps echoed behind us. I glanced to see him following us. Steven and I quickened our gait. The man's footsteps were slower than ours, probably because of his smoking habit. I said a silent prayer of gratitude for our fitness level.

As we steadily climbed the Tor's steep pathway, I felt perspiration under my layers of clothing. We climbed the stairs until they turned into a straight passage leading up to the tower.

In the darkness surrounded by the mist, I again felt an ominous sensation. I thought of 80-year-old Abbot Whiting, who'd been hung and beheaded atop the Tor's tower during King Henry VIII's roundup of monastery wealth. For a moment, I wondered whether the abbot haunted his place of death, but then immediately realized that his spirit stayed at the abbey below the Tor.

No, the tower was safe, since it was dedicated to, and protected by, Archangel Michael.

Still, I felt nervous as we approached the tower, feeling the presence of people there and wondering what to expect. A coven of witches? A Druid circle? What right did we (meaning Steven and myself) have to encroach upon their ancient ceremonial grounds? As Steven and I reached the top of the Tor, we saw darkly dressed people sitting in a circle in front of the tower. My husband walked boldly toward them, and I followed timidly but steadily. As soon as we got close, the veil of fear dropped when we discovered that they were a group of young people passing around a marijuana cigarette!

Inside Michael's tower, people slumbered in sleeping bags. We walked to the south side of the structure to escape the biting-cold wind. I heard a rumbling sound, which turned out to be a man snoring loudly! Steven and I giggled. So much for our big Beltaine plans!

We walked to a bench just below the tower and sat down. The mist surrounding the Tor made it appear to be surrounded by a large body of water. I could see Avalon clearly, and Glastonbury disappeared behind the mists. So this was why we trekked up the Tor in the middle of the night—twilight was when Avalon revealed itself!

A rooster crowed in the distance as the sun crept toward the horizon, and the sky was a bright cobalt blue. The gorgeous deep color reminded me of the glow that I see around Archangel Michael.

As we walked down the hill, a voice said, *"There's no shame in feeling fear or nervousness. It's what you do with those emotions that matters most. Facing your fears as you've been doing is the initiation into priestesshood. Anyone wishing to be a priestess must do the same and face her fears as well."*

By facing my fears, I'd been initiated.

Beltaine at Chalice Well

Steven and I walked from the Tor to Chalice Well, where a Beltaine ceremony was scheduled to begin at 5 A.M. A long line of people waited in the parking lot for the gates to open, and I enjoyed looking at the variety of gowns and cloaks that the participants wore. Most had viney flower wreaths on their heads, celebrating the coming springtime.

A tall woman dressed in a long lavender gown and a man wearing an emerald cape led us all to the lower springs of Chalice Well. This area had just been reconstructed with a beautiful Vesica Piscis shape (two intersecting circles with a fish shape at the core of their intersection) outlined in brick. Our hosts welcomed us and said that Beltaine was the marriage and union of opposites: fire and water, God and Goddess, male and female.

They passed around a basket of dark green floatable candles. We were instructed to hold an intention or make a wish and then light the candle and float it in the intersecting portion of the two Vesica Piscis circles. Since that section was symbolic of a vulva, it was a portal to the creation of our intentions.

Candles floating in the Chalice Well Beltaine ceremony.

I desired that my heart be more open to love, so I lit the candle and set it in the intersecting circles. My candle floated among those lit by the other participants, and the candlelight reflected beautifully upon the water as our hosts escorted us all to the meadows of Chalice Well. The long grass was damp and cold, and Steven wrapped his arms and cape around me to keep me warm. The other people seemed impervious to the cold, undoubtedly from years of acclimation.

We faced east to welcome the light on this first day of summer. A man associated with our hosts invoked the male Celtic sun deities Bel and Apollo, and his female partner invoked the Celtic sun goddesses Sulis and Brigit.

The couple then lit a flame beneath a pile of lumber in the center of the meadow. Unlike the previous evening's lighted coals in the Goddess Temple courtyard, this morning there was a large bonfire. I wondered how we'd jump over it without setting ourselves ablaze.

I watched a woman who stood near us at the ceremony. She had the dark, stern, brooding energy of the goddess Vivien of Avalon. I thought of how many powerful women I'd met with the same intimidating char-

The Beltaine bonfire at Chalice Well.

acteristics. But intimidation wasn't the sort of power I wanted to develop.

Vivien represents the Matriarch aspect of the goddess, yet the other triple goddess aspects (the Maiden and the Mother) are just as powerful. Priestesses take many forms, and I vowed to develop a nurturing and loving Matriarch aspect within myself as I aged.

Back at the inn, Steven and I dined with a pleasant older woman named Mary Jo who'd also attended the Beltaine ceremony. Her carefully chosen words revealed a well-read and thoughtful woman. *Here is an example of a powerful and lovable Matriarch!* I thought.

Mary Jo said that she'd jumped the Beltaine fire to erase old energy from her past. She said cryptically, "I'm mad for spirituality but don't care for religion at all."

Steven and I looked at each other. Why would this pleasant, grandmotherly looking woman make such a sweeping statement? After all, didn't religion often offer comfort, community, and guidance? It wasn't for everyone, but didn't it provide answers for millions of people?

Mary Jo then explained why she distrusted formal religion: "I entered a convent and became a nun in the 1960s and left in the '80s. During that time, I saw and experienced so many abuses and so much hypocrisy that I had a breakdown. Now I realize that my breakdown was a blessing because it led me to leave the convent.

"During my 20 years there, I became completely out of touch with the world. I regret that now, because the nuns (including myself) made grievous errors while teaching children in Catholic school. The world changed so drastically while I was in the convent that it took me a while to deal with everything when I left. Today, I keep up on world events." Mary Jo then engaged in a brief, lively discussion of American politics with me, which proved her point.

She then added, "I believe people turn to religion because they're afraid of their own spiritual power, so they give it away to priests, rabbis, churches, and temples."

Mary Jo now teaches classes about life transitions.

While I still believe that religion serves an important purpose for many, I understood Mary Jo's feelings. I think that if you're going to learn from spiritual teachers and religious figures, it's important not to assume that they have more power than you do, or are superior to you in any way. You must pay attention to your inner guidance and only listen to the messages that ring true for you.

Looking at Mary Jo, you'd never guess that beneath her conservative dress, minimal makeup, and shortly cropped gray hair . . . she's a very powerful goddess indeed.

✻ ✻ ✻ ✻ ✻ ✻

Chapter 17

GODDESSES, ANGELS, AND THE RAINBOW CHILDREN

Refreshed after Glastonbury, Steven and I returned to London, where I was scheduled to give a series of lectures. At our hotel concierge's suggestion, we decided to have dinner at a Thai restaurant called the Mango Tree. We followed the concierge's directions, but the restaurant was nowhere in sight. We kept walking until the street came to a dead end at Victoria Station.

I prayed aloud for Archangel Chamuel to help us find the restaurant. Chamuel's name means "He who sees God," and he's brilliant at seeing anything that seems to be lost . . . which we were at that moment. Right after saying the prayer, I noticed a cab driver sitting and eating in his parked car. I asked if he knew the location of the Mango Tree restaurant.

"Never heard of it," he said sweetly. He strained to figure out where the restaurant might be located, but couldn't remember seeing it. We thanked him and walked back toward our hotel. Five minutes later, a car horn caught our attention. It was the cab driver! He'd found the Mango Tree and had come to find us to tell us of its location. We offered to pay him for his help, but he refused to take any money.

As we settled into our table at the Mango Tree, I silently thanked the cab driver and Archangel Chamuel. Angels come in many forms, including disguised as London taxi drivers.

Rainbow Children and the Merpeople

The next day, May 4, was both a full moon and a lunar eclipse, *and* it was Buddha's birthday, which is sometimes called *Wesak* (pronounced *WEE-sock*). So the energy at St. James Church in Piccadilly Circus seemed magical that evening as the audience assembled for my annual discussion of the angels' messages sponsored by the nonprofit group Alternatives. As I sat backstage, Archangel Metatron (who oversees the Indigo, Crystal, and Rainbow children) urged me to write his message and then read it aloud to the audience:

"The Children of the Rainbow are being assembled and prepared for a mass influx among the population. They are multidimensional, holographic beings filled with love, without being ruled by ego-based emotions. They are wise without being overly intellectual. They are unconcerned with impressing others or competition of any kind.

"They see and recognize only love, like angels. Parents must avoid the temptation to burden these children by making them confidants, as the Children of the Rainbow are excellent listeners and very compassionate.

"Yes, some of them are here on Earth, born in emotionally warm and open countries, particularly Mexico, Italy, Chile, Peru, Venezuela, New Zealand, Australia, and parts of Africa and Eastern Europe.

"The Crystal Children are the primary conduits for the Rainbow energy, in the same way that crystals reflect light into rainbow prisms. This ultra-healing energy is pouring into the planets' airwaves, radio frequencies, and water to disperse the energies and soak the planet and population in them. Dolphins, Reiki-attuned people, and merpeople are also dispersing the rainbow energy right now.

"The way to bring more rainbow healing energy to the planet is through its dissemination in human bodies, known as Children of the Rainbow. This energy has only previously been embodied in the form of dolphins. Like other areas of human evolution, it's now moving from the water onto dry land. You need fire as light through the prism of water to illuminate the rainbow rays."

Metatron's words reminded me of Lisa Weiss's dream in which the dolphins told her they'd be returning to take over the earth. *Could the new Rainbow Children be from the dolphin realm?* I wondered. After I relayed Metatron's message to the audience, I turned my attention to Archangel Raziel (the wizard archangel who knows and teaches all of the spiritual secrets and esoteric wisdom). "Tell us more about the connection between dolphins, mermaids, and humans," I implored.

He replied immediately: *"They're simultaneous beings who co-exist in different dimensions, depending upon where your focus is directed. If you only focus upon dolphins, that's all you'll see, but if you look holographically at the energy of dolphins, you'll see their energy grids, as well as the humans merged with dolphins, who are the merpeople, and the dolphins merged with angels, who are the merangels.*

"The rainbow spectrum will increase the human brain's serotonin levels, in the same way that the rainbow rays within natural sunlight act as antidepressants. You were given rainbows within light to feed and to illuminate your inner rainbow of chakras. That's why you need sunshine to stay bright and healthy.

"The archangels don't have the red ray of light, so we cannot give you the full rainbow spectrum ourselves. The goddesses hold the red ray, particularly the fire goddesses Pele and Brigit. The goddess Quan Yin holds a cherry-red ray that reflects the beautiful and peaceful side of fire in the form of devotion. So by working with us archangels and the goddesses, you absorb rainbow energy, which helps you feel better, physically and emotionally.

"Water has memory and holds energy. That's why the water at Lourdes, Brigit's Well, Chalice Well, and other healing wells has powerful effects. The water is imbued with the loving energy of goddesses and angels, as well as with prayers offered by people asking for healing. Water is rainbow droplets that heal in the same way crystal prisms focus light into rainbow spectrums."

In the book-signing line following the talk, a woman brought her three-year-old daughter to see me. "Her name is Ariana," the mother said as she placed the wide-eyed, dark-skinned girl on my desk so that we were face-to-face.

Ariana's penetrating gaze led me to first believe that she was a Crystal Child, but I noticed a fearlessness not found in these young ones (who are generally quite shy). Like a Crystal Child, she spoke to me telepathically. The average person would have assumed that she wasn't speaking at all.

Ariana leaned her forehead against mine so our third eyes touched. My mind's eye filled with images of dolphins as this amazing child downloaded visions and information to me about humans stopping ecological abuses. Her telepathic movie and message continued for quite some time until I became aware of the long line of people waiting for me to sign their books.

I was emotionally moved by Ariana's presence and message. She was a wise old soul in a tiny body—a Matriarch goddess at the age of three. A true Rainbow Child, she hadn't flinched, fussed, or cried during our entire time together. Instead, she demonstrated the remarkable new rainbow energy, which is about giving, while being unconcerned with receiving.

Healing Old Fears

After we returned to our hotel, Steven read aloud from *The Way of Wyrd* (Hay House), a book about ancient Celtic shamanism. It's the story of a Christian crusader who infiltrates a pagan Anglo-Saxon community to gain inside information about them. The reader learns about ancient shamanism through the eyes of the crusader, who eventually becomes sympathetic to shamanism.

As Steven read, I suddenly feared that I wasn't acknowledging God and Jesus enough. The feelings weren't based on a healthy longing for the love of God or Jesus—they were deep-seated, ancient fears about being punished for breaking religious rules. My breath deepened as I tapped in to pain from centuries of religious persecution and punishment, including my own from prior lifetimes.

Just that evening, two audience members asked why I hadn't mentioned God or Jesus during my talk. Ordinarily I frequently speak about the Creator and the ascended master, Jesus. But that evening's talk had focused more upon archangels and Buddhist ascended masters in honor of Buddha's birthday. The two audience members' confrontational questions seemed based upon their personal insecurities about being punished for breaking a religious rule.

Are we all operating out of this same old fear? I wondered. *If so, how can we collectively get over it as soon as possible?*

So many of us behaved like unhealed abuse survivors who'd become depressed and helpless, and who'd given up our personal power. I asked God, Jesus, and the angels to give us all a solution so we could forgive and heal.

As I fell asleep, a comforting voice said to me, *"When you take off your armor, you find and experience amour."* As always, the solution was love and faith. I asked for the courage to drop my protective defenses so I could feel love on an even deeper and more consistent level.

✳✳✳✳✳✳

Chapter 18

HEALING WATERS

Steven and I had traveled to Dublin, Ireland, as part of our book tour, and I wanted to use the hotel gym before giving my daylong workshop. I'd timed everything precisely, arriving there when it opened, which would allow me an hour's workout. The one thing I hadn't planned was that it would be closed and locked when I arrived.

I asked Archangel Michael to help me: "Please let the person in charge of opening this gym get through traffic and arrive here on time."

Michael replied, *"Don't tell me how to get the gym open. Just visualize it being open."* So I did, and instantly a man appeared from a back room to unlock the door. The man hadn't been stuck in traffic at all, as my imagination had implied—he had just been in the back room! Archangel Michael helped me focus only on *what* I desired to manifest, instead of trying to figure out *how* to get it. I had a great workout, which definitely supported me in giving the sold-out seminar to 800 people that day.

While teaching the course, Archangel Michael told me, *"Everyone <u>wants</u> to detox. They just need the courage, strength, and motivation to do so."* I asked Michael to speak through me to the audience, and he said, *"You may believe that your angels are trying to ruin your fun by asking you to change your diet and lifestyle, but they are actually are guiding you to a higher energy level in answer to your prayers. They know that the simplest way to raise your frequency is for* *you to avoid low-frequency foods and beverages such as sugar, white flour, meat, alcohol, caffeine, nicotine, and dairy products. The angels can eliminate or reduce your cravings for these substances if you just ask for and accept their help."*

Fire and Water

After the workshop, Steven and I drove with an Irish friend of ours named Fiona McClelland and our British friend and editor, Michelle Pilley, to see Brigit's Well. The healing well was built on the site of Brigit's former cathedral in the town of Kildare outside of Dublin.

How interesting that a fire goddess has a water well, I thought during the drive. We pulled onto an unpaved country road, and a

small sign pointed us to a beautiful little fenced park containing Brigit's Well. The park had a river and a statue of Brigit, which portrayed her much more conservatively than I'd experienced and seen her.

The park's energy echoed its centuries as a place of refuge, comfort, and healing.

Brigit's Well in Ireland.

I closed my eyes to connect with Brigit, and asked her to tell me about the elements of fire and water.

Brigit's powerful yet feminine voice spoke to me immediately with the clearest connection I'd yet had with her: *"Fire is the essence of the inner light, the eternal burning passion to do service in the name of love.*

"Invoke the flame to motivate you, to lift your courage and strength, to purify your motivations, and to energize and invigorate you. Tell people when they invoke the flame that they won't need to caffeinate

themselves. They can be naturally aroused and invigorated by spending time in meditation each morning before they arise or just after arising (very important). Just like a sunrise, their fire will be lit, and they won't need artificial means to stoke their inner flames.

"*If people would instill the habit of invoking their inner fire upon awakening, they wouldn't rush into action immediately and expect themselves to be instantly charged, and thereby in need of artificial means for energy inducement.*

"*Women in particular have cold extremities, which is tied in to a lack of courage. So they especially need to invoke and stoke their inner flames. This will bring more courage, stamina, and resilience to their energy fields, more passion into their lives, and more of a reason to stay alive.*"

I asked her, "Brigit, why are you also associated with water?"

She replied, "*The early folks dedicated this well to me out of kindly respect and love for some of the healings I'd been involved in, and also because they feared fire. The water is more associated with the feminine, yet I have a fiery spirit—and I'm entirely female. Everyone who knew me as a mortal spoke about what they labeled as my temper, but by today's standards, my disposition would be considered mild. The truth is that my ire was raised by ill treatment of the children, and of this land by governments and other institutions of royal power. Members of the reigning powers would collectively decide what was 'in our best interests,' and I wasn't so keen on government rule, especially when it diminished our capacity to feed our children. Grain restrictions and other covenants were the theme of the time when I lived as a mortal.*"

I asked Brigit whether healings had occurred at her well.

"*Of course!*" she replied. "*The prayers within water purify, bless, and invigorate it with extra-healing capacity.*"

Then she spoke slowly and deliberately: "*Prayer is fire, and praying over water is a way to fuse and merge the two elements. You also have earth below the stream here, and plenty of air. This sanctuary is a place of perfect balance of the four elements, with Spirit here from the faith and expectations of all who visit. Please tell people to come here and visit my well so that it may continue to flourish.*"

I walked over to Brigit's well, a stone-encircled container of dark, still water from deep within the ground. I touched the water, and felt great power and energy surge through my fingers, all the way into my body.

As we left the park, we paused at a stone temple where a boy was kneeling and praying before a lighted candle. Brigit's words echoed in my mind: *"Prayer is fire."*

That night Steven and I were so relaxed that we could have fallen asleep before dinnertime. I felt fed, nourished, and nurtured by Brigit. As I was drifting asleep, a voice said to me, *"The wells keep you well."*

Lourdes

Two days after our visit to Brigit's Well, Steven and I were in a small airplane en route from Paris to Lourdes. I'd been warned that the flight to Lourdes might be depressing because of the seriously ill passengers we'd see on the plane. But the opposite was true: There was a lighthearted, adventurous spirit among our small group on the Air France Fokker 100 airplane.

Our fellow passengers consisted of two priests dressed in full regalia, young mothers with children, several couples, a few backpackers, and a woman lavishly dressed in fur and diamonds. Everyone seemed happy and enthused—in fact, our anticipation reminded me of people waiting in line for an amusement-park ride. We were all excited about connecting with the Holy Mother. As the small airplane took off, I had the ironic thought: *Well, if our plane crashes, we'll all definitely see Mary.* Yet I knew that we were safe and protected on this true spiritual pilgrimage.

Looking out the window, I marveled at the pyramid shape of the Pyrenees mountains. Then I gasped as I realized the connection between the word *pyramids* and *Pyrenees.* The prefix *pyr* means "fire" in Greek. Another reference to fire, just as we were traveling to the water of Lourdes!

We landed and hailed a taxi. "The energy of Lourdes is wonderful," Steven remarked, as we rode to our hotel. "It feels so loving and peaceful here." The verdant hills, fresh air, and quaint buildings made us feel as if we'd taken a time machine into another century. There was a simplicity to the valley's beauty, which was decorated with breathtakingly beautiful springtime flowers.

However, upon arriving in Lourdes, we saw the first of hundreds of commercial stands crowded into every square foot possible. Each flea-market-style booth was crammed with products bearing images of Mother Mary, St. Bernadette, and Jesus. We saw Jesus clocks, giant glow-in-the dark rosaries, St. Bernadette capes, and Mother Mary snow globes. And everywhere we looked, vendors sold Mother Mary water bottles to fill at the Lourdes well.

The hotels in the village were old and small. We'd chosen the highest-rated hotel in the travel books, yet it was dark and cramped. Signs hung in our bathroom saying DO NOT DISPOSE OF SYRINGES IN THE TRASH CAN. Lourdes hotels were apparently accustomed to patrons in desperate health conditions. At least our room had windows that opened to dazzling views of the Pyrenees mountains. Part of Lourdes's sweetness was the feminine Mother Mary and Bernadette energy, mixed with its vibrant natural surroundings.

Steven and I walked to St. Bernadette's family home, now a historical monument. I was shocked by the size of the single-room dwelling, which had housed Bernadette, her sister, two brothers, and her mother and father. When the family became destitute, a cousin allowed them to stay in this 12-square-foot *Cahot,* or abandoned prison cell. The room had no bathroom, kitchen, or sink—just four walls and a fireplace. It was so small that if you put

Sitting in Bernadette's Cahot.

a king-sized bed in the room, you'd barely have room to walk, and yet a family of six had lived there.

The energy of Bernadette's miracles and the prayers of pilgrim travelers hung in the room. I felt humbled by the future saint's meager existence, especially after learning that she never complained. In fact, reports say that she frequently expressed gratitude for what she *did* have.

From Bernadette's Cahot, we walked to the Lourdes grotto. I was surprised to see an elaborate basilica surrounding it. It looked like an ostentatious European castle, too overdressed for the humble surroundings of Lourdes, or Bernadette's impoverished upbringing.

I felt angry on behalf of Bernadette, who was persecuted and scorned by the Lourdes church and government while experiencing her visions of "The Lady." Yet she'd loved the church and was a devoted nun for the remainder of her life. I felt that Bernadette had let go of resentment toward the church and government, if she'd ever held any in the first place. I decided to also forgive those who'd spiritually persecuted me in previous lifetimes, and let go of the attendant pain.

The Grotto

Steven and I walked straight past the basilica and headed toward the grotto where Mary had instructed Bernadette to dig in the dirt, and where the healing well had sprung up as a result. As we neared the grotto, we saw hundreds of people wearing blue Windbreakers and red armbands pushing people in wheelchairs. They were headed toward the basilica for the daily Blessing of the Sick ritual.

The grotto was fenced off, so you had to stand in a line to walk past it. As we waited our turn, I looked at the brilliant statue of the Holy Mother standing on the wet, dark ledge where Bernadette had seen her. The statue wore a white gown and blue girdle with golden roses at her feet, just as Bernadette had described in her visions. A sign in French below Mary read: I AM THE IMMACULATE CONCEPTION, which is how the lady identified herself to Bernadette at the Massabielle grotto.

The line to enter the Lourdes Grotto.

I was completely unprepared for the powerful energy of the healing well within the grotto. The sensation was stronger and more intense than anything I'd experienced on Earth. I felt as if I'd just crossed over and was with the angels! My head pounded and my eyes rolled spontaneously, as if I were traveling at high velocity. I felt like crying—not from pain, but from the pure beauty of the powerful maternal love surrounding the well.

I knew that Mother Mary was everywhere on Earth, but the healing well was definitely a focal point, with the energy of a billion angels. I floated on air with pure bliss and euphoria. If there hadn't been people in line behind me, I would have stayed there for hours. I walked to the seating area in front of the grotto and began crying. Such sweet, pure, loving, and ecstatically nurturing energy!

After I recovered, Steven and I walked through the line again. The second time was even more powerful. I had a vision of walking through a waterfall of purifying healing energy. My feelings of inner peace and bliss defied description.

That night I felt tired but happy, just as I had after experiencing Brigit's Well. I was nourished and well mothered, which seemed especially fitting considering that the day before had been Mother's Day! That night I dreamed I wore a swan outfit and could fly.

We returned to the grotto early the next morning, and I went through the line to stand by the water well several times. Each time, old layers of fear, anger, sarcasm, bitterness, and emotional scars were washed away by the angelic waterfall of healing energy within the grotto walls.

I sat down on the benches facing the grotto to have a conversation with Mary. Although I didn't see her, I certainly felt her presence and could hear her voice. I asked her to elaborate on the request she'd given me during my crystal-healing bed session.

"How can I help the children?" I asked.

Her sweet voice came quickly, and I wrote down her words: *"All prayers lead to success. Keep your prayers continually fresh, active, and alive. Do not lapse into prayer for prayer's sake, or prayer as a simple habit (especially to assuage guilt).*

"Prayer is a necessity on the planet, and you feel its energy strongly here. It is fresh, awake, and alive because people arrive here in Lourdes without expectations other than to be healed from their present aching and reality. Many of them are desperate for cures, guidance, answers, and miracles.

"Many are reticent to ask for such favors for themselves, but will gladly ask on behalf of someone they love dearly. Their faces become clear as candlelight, and they know exactly what they want (such as a healing), and they demonstrate healing by casting their thoughts as prayers toward me, Heaven, and toward the nurses and priests who are here.

"The passion, intensity, fervor, and focus of their prayers ignite them into action. Intensified and clarified prayer is what leads to healing. You cannot force a healing, but you can reveal one. Do not be afraid of experiencing miracles. Accept them good-naturedly with gratitude, in the way that a baby is glad when his mother feeds him.

"Cast all fears, doubt, and naysaying in the other direction, and put your focus wholly in the light, which is represented here by many candles. These flames bring awareness of the holy fire within and surrounding each and every one of you.

"As to the children, reach for them inside as well. Light candles on their behalf literally and metaphorically. Illuminate their path with light.

"To all adults: Take your role as caretakers of the children very seriously, for it is imbued with Heaven's blessings, which shall oversee the upliftment of all of your fellow men (female, male, and children). The children especially need and require extra shepherding at this confusing time on the planet.

"Far too much violence is available like a ticking time bomb for the children. It is horrifying that this violence is viewed as entertainment and marketed in this way. From our perspective, violence in children's entertainment creates flames of rage in their hearts—a rage that already exists and threatens to run out of control like a forest fire. The entertainment industry must either be reigned in, or parents must cease to whet their children's appetites for violence by not indulging in it as well.

"Blessing and purifying your own body and the children's bodies is the heart of the solution. As their hearts are assimilated with the beautiful magic of pure maternal love, their hearts grow in softness and sweetness. This increased sensitivity then reduces the appetite for violence, including internal violence toward the self in forms such as self-degradation, and external forms such as acting out in violence.

"The children _must_ be saved from gang violence, violence in the media, and violence in households. Violence is the acting out of the darkest poison within human souls. Let the children bathe in my waters to purify and bless their souls.

"Give the children water that is prayed over, either from here in Massabielle, or even better, from a parent's pure and sweet intentions infused into the child's drinking glass. Shine your light like a beacon upon your children, parents. Do not be afraid to speak of your truth to your children. They will appreciate your time and efforts devoted to truth. This will herald a new golden age, when more parents will take the time to speak honestly with heart to their children.

"Today's children are natural curiosity seekers, and they thirst for tradition in family matters, hunger for a spiritual basis in life, and deeply need their parents to be way-showers. In your youth-obsessed culture, far too many parents want to behave like adolescents and don't want to face aging and maturity. They don't want to grow up. This is having devastating effects on your youths, who need mature leaders to steer their way. Parents, grow up and stop acting like overgrown teenagers! Stop being your child's peer, and be their guardian instead.

"Love, love, love them enough to be way-showers, which begins with infusing yourself with the strength to be a steady role model—not *on-again, off-again, but a consistent role model who lives a life of compassion, courage, and respect for self, life, and others.*

"Magnify the purification effect of prayers by blessing your food and water before they are consumed. Do this for your children, your children's children, and for your pets. Your scientists will soon bear out the powerful practice of prayers and tones upon water. The prayers and blessings undo many of the effects of toxins in your body and environment. The starlight normally illuminates your waters with uplifting energy. However, the dirt in your air has reduced the effect of starlight reaching your waters, so hands-on healing, which contains the same light as comes from the stars, is similar enough to have the same effects of recharging the water.

"Hold the bottle or glass of water in your hands and pray over it briefly. Call upon my name if you choose, and I will join my energies with your own."

The Candlelight Procession

At 9 P.M., Steven and I joined about 7,000 other people at the basilica courtyard for the outdoor candlelight procession, which is held nightly from April through October. Each person held a foot-long white tapered candle, housed in a paper cup that shielded the hands from the flame. Images of St. Bernadette and Mother Mary, and the words to hymns in French and English, were printed on each paper cup.

A man and a woman said prayers in French, English, German, and Spanish over the loudspeaker system as we all slowly walked, five people wide, along the courtyard walkways. Everyone held their candles above their head whenever we'd sing the chorus: "Ave, Ave, Ave Maria" in a beautiful display of candlelight and united voices.

Ahead of us in the procession, a young Crystal Child popped out of her stroller. She ran to comfort an elderly man pushing his wife in a wheelchair. Her mother retrieved the girl and forced her back into her stroller. The little girl protested loudly. She wanted to comfort the man! Like many Crystal Children, her heart was dialed to the setting of compassion, healing, and helpfulness.

As I fell asleep that night, I asked Mary, "Why can't all the world feel as wonderful as the energy of the grotto?"

When I woke up, I heard the answer: *"Because water is magnetic, and this water is infused with fervent prayer. That is the difference. Prayer that is fervent is intensified with emotion and is electrically charged. Water is magnetic and holds electrical charges in suspension. That is how homeopathy and dowsing work."*

Since our flight didn't leave for Paris until that afternoon, Steven and I were able to visit the grotto in the morning. I was so excited to be in its nurturing energy again. I purchased a perfect white rosebud at a booth outside the Basilica, and as we waited in line to approach the healing well, I prayed into the rose for all children. I also prayed, "Please help me to help the children. Please help me to clearly hear, feel, see, and know the messages about the children that need to be delivered."

As we approached the healing well, its energy once again enveloped me like the loving embrace of a thousand angels. *This must be what it feels like to have a near-death experience,* I thought. First, I felt the energy in my head, as a pressure and pleasantly enveloping sensation, followed by a deep warmth in my heart, and then tingling in my body. My heart beat faster as the line crept closer to the Beloved One.

I touched the water streaming from the grotto rocks and put it on my third eye, ear, and crown chakras. Then I placed the white rose inside the grotto fence near the healing well—a very powerful place for my prayers for the children to be heard, and, I was certain, to be answered! Then, as I approached the healing well, I saw an image of Mary in my mind's eye, and a voice cried excitedly, *"She is here! She is arisen!"*

The word *arisen* seemed more reserved for describing Jesus' ascension, but the voice said, *"'She is arisen' refers to the rising mother, the reawakening feminine."* Then I saw a vision of a dawning sun.

I asked Mary, "What else would you like me to know, write, or teach about?"

In her sweet yet powerful voice, she replied, *"Spread the word of the dawning new light. It is ancient, yet it is new. The tides are turning on a new phase of life itself. A new sanity will reign once more, heralded in by this new light of maternity that is bequeathing humanity with a reawakening of a new sensibility. This is the dawning of true compassion, mixed with leadership, where the feminine will reign once more.*

"True equality comes from compassion, which is touching and feeling the Divine within yourself and every person. To truly touch the Divine, you must feel compassion toward each and every person, and not be selective in whom you will cast your blessings upon. This is the true meaning of a spiritual movement, when you move accordingly.

"Action is now needed more than anything. Divinely directed action is the meaning of the movement. Shine the light of utter and complete compassion upon everyone. Don't leave anyone out, even those who seem to treat you badly or tread upon you. These are beings who are the most in need of your compassionate understanding."

Her phrase "compassionate understanding" intrigued me, and I asked her to expand upon its meaning. She explained, *"It means to feel the understanding and forgiveness toward another, instead of just intellectually understanding."*

Then she continued with her message: *"The blissful and peaceful energies of the grotto will travel and settle throughout the globe. The maternal will be the new leader. Just as a mother knows what's best for her family and must delegate chores, so must all mothers delegate what to do to save the big family of the world.*

"Follow my lead and be a strong, purified, and loving leader. No longer forsake the feminine, especially the Mother. Peace be to you who try to help one another, for I shall be there in your midst. Retain your hopefulness and your faith, for I promise you a new dawning upon the morrow, a new sun of reigning maternal love. Just as in a family, the Mother instinctively knows what to do; she knows the answers. And then a wise woman asks for help from other family members. She asks her strong husband and sons to accomplish that which requires muscle, and she asks her intellectual daughter to do that which requires writing or arithmetic. She directs her household with the wisdom only a Mother possesses.

(I don't believe that Mary necessarily meant a woman had to give birth to have the Mother wisdom. I felt that she also meant that women have this Mothering wisdom inherent within them.)

"Strength of leadership, the courage to stand up and teach as Bernadette displayed, and the Mother wisdom are sorely needed right now. Will you pick up this sword? Will you accept this assignment? (I felt Mary speaking to all of us.) *The time is ripe for conviction within leadership. Choose a life of integrity, wisdom, compassion, and leadership. Do this for me and for each other, caring not at all for personal gain, but instead for personal growth.*

"You have all that you need. Have faith that more will be provided along the way, much as my son displayed in his earthly days. May everyone find what they are looking for, and know that there is plenty for all."

Putting Compassion into Action

As I wrote down Mary's words, a middle-aged woman with short hair and a faded red jacket sat next to me and physically pushed me, so I scooted to the right. I was surprised, as everyone sitting on the bench had seemed so respectful of each other's space until this woman shoved me. I figured that she wanted to make room for the Catholic priest sitting to her left, so I scooted over again to give her even more room.

I didn't think any more about her until awhile later when Steven and I were standing against a gate next to the line for the grotto. As Steven wrote in his journal, the woman walked by and uttered a very loud, disdainful grunt. I looked up and noticed that it was the same woman from the bench. I didn't think any more of it until Steven said, "Was she saying that as a judgment of us?" I replied, "Well, that was my first impression, too."

I looked the woman in the eye, and she looked back at me blankly with no indication of either malice or joy. Just blank. She probably was just "that way," I decided, either because of her personality or an illness, or having someone else in her life who was ill.

But I allowed her to upset me for a time. My ego took full advantage and began sending me doubts: *What if I'm wrong for being here as a non-Catholic? Who am I to talk with Mother Mary?*

I asked the Holy Mother to please purify me, and to let me know if I was erring in any way. I then remembered her words about total and absolute compassion. I needed to love this woman who had triggered pain in me. There were 7,000 pleasant people around me at the grotto, and I was allowing one woman who wasn't to pull me out of my peaceful bliss!

Then I thought about Bernadette. Almost everyone—family, peers, clergy, and legal authorities—had angrily judged her during her visions, yet Bernadette had stood by her experiences. She lovingly spoke her truth without losing her peace. Bernadette didn't care if others believed her; she just wanted to be allowed to visit the grotto and see the Lady.

I thought of the history of religious and spiritual persecution and the words in *A Course in Miracles:* "A universal theology is impossible, but a universal experience is not only possible but necessary." Someday we'll all realize that we're talking about the same Creator through various religious and spiritual paths, even though we use different words to describe the experience.

I walked through the grotto to the healing well again, putting more water on my third eye, heart, ear, and crown chakras. As I neared the well, I walked through a shower of tremendous healing energy. I felt big love in my heart, purified of anger or judgment toward the woman and all she represented. I walked away with a big smile and bliss in my heart.

Many of the people who come to Lourdes may not have their conditions cured, but they become visibly peaceful as their wheelchairs and gurneys are pushed past the grotto and their nurses place water from the grotto rocks upon their heads. They could, at least, be healed of mental and emotional suffering. As Steven and I walked out of the basilica gates, he remarked, "They may not all be *cured,* but everyone who comes to Lourdes is *healed.*"

✸✸✸✸✸✸

Chapter 19

LIVING GODDESSES

As Steven and I returned to Paris, we saw a small version of the Statue of Liberty standing by the Seine River. That's when I realized that the most significant symbol of the United States is of a goddess holding a flame!

French Freemasons gifted the statue to their American brothers in honor of this country, which was built upon Masonic principles. The Freemasons' foundations go back to the ancient principles of King Solomon, which include the recognition of the feminine and masculine aspects of God.

Both the sculptor and engineer who worked on the Statue of Liberty were French Freemasons who used the Egyptian goddess Isis as their model. The statue was originally conceived as a gateway symbol for the opening of the Suez Canal. When it was rejected for that purpose, the sculptor renamed the statue "Liberty" after the goddess of the same name, and presented it to the United States. A smaller version stands by the Seine River in Paris. Incidentally, the Seine is named for the Roman-Celtic river goddess, Sequana, who heals with the water of her river.

As Chancellor of England, Sir Francis Bacon (a Freemason and author of the book *New Atlantis*) helped to create the American colony of Virginia. Bacon left his mark by placing the goddess Virtus on the Virginia flag. Goddess images abound in the United States, including Athena on the state flag of California and a mosaic of Minerva in the Library of Congress in Washington, D.C.

That afternoon, Steven and I walked through the Louvre museum. I marveled as we stood beneath the giant statues of Grecian and Roman goddesses such as Artemis, Athena, and Aphrodite. Perhaps the most famous statue is that of Nike, a goddess with angel wings.

As we left the Louvre, we passed by a statue erected in honor of France's patron saint, Joan of Arc. At the age of 14, this uneducated farm girl received messages from Archangel Michael and St. Catherine to save France from British invasions. Filled with doubts, Joan followed this Divine guidance and led an army, which ensured France's independence. Her supporters believed an ancient prophecy that foretold of a Maiden of Lorraine, France, who would save the country. Joan the Maiden lived very near the Province of Lorraine, and her life mirrored the prophecy.

Soon after she helped Charles gain the throne of France, he sold Joan to the British, who tried her for treason and heresy. She was burned at the stake when she refused to deny the voices of angels and saints. I wonder if today Joan would have been labeled with Attention Deficit Disorder and placed on Ritalin for her activism. She truly was a front-runner among Indigo Children, along with Bernadette.

The Inquisitors who burned Joan of Arc called her a heathen, which originally meant someone who dwelled on the heath or wild, open country. Similarly, the term *pagan* originally meant "country dweller." I found it interesting that both Joan of Arc and St. Bernadette, who were so highly attuned to Divine guidance, lived in the countryside.

Being outside in nature opens our spiritual gifts and helps us notice Spirit's life force within trees, rivers, plants, animals, and stones. The Inquisitors were older men from cities who worshiped in dark, enclosed buildings. Perhaps if they'd gone outside more often, they would have realized the truths of which the "heathen" spoke.

Even today, we ridicule country-dwellers with labels such as "hick," "country bumpkin," and "hillbilly." Those terms aren't far removed from the phrases now associated with darkness, because of the Inquisitions: "heathen" and "pagan." Heathen and pagans, though, are simply people who find their connection with the Divine outside in nature. Who among us couldn't fit that definition?

Signs from Venus

I had been getting lots of signs about Venus. It seemed that everywhere I turned, I read or heard something that mentioned it. At first I wrote it off as coincidence, but it became increasingly clear that this was a *sign*. But what did it mean beyond its ancient association with the Divine feminine? Finally, one morning I asked in prayer to be shown the meaning.

An hour later, I felt directed to the Internet and discovered that on June 8, 2004, there would be a Venus transit that would eclipse the sun. With Venus being symbolic of feminine energy, and the sun the historic male-energy symbol, this solar eclipse was significant.

The Venus solar eclipse had only occurred four times since the telescope was invented and wouldn't happen again until 2012. I thought of how I'd seen the image of the planet Venus carved into the building next to the pyramid in Chichén Itzá, and in my vision while sitting on the pyramid steps. Perhaps this was why the Mayan calendar ended in 2012. . . .

I felt guided to lead a peace prayer on the evening of the Venus transit, to invite the goddess to return. At first I thought, *Well I can just do a private ceremony at home or at the beach.* Then I felt pushed to have a public gathering, so I contacted the Goddess Temple of Orange County (O.C.).

An old friend of mine, Ava Park, whom I'd met through the O.C. People for Animals, had recently opened the Goddess Temple. She agreed to hold the Venus Transit ceremony at her temple, to honor and invite the goddess to return and balance the male patriarchal energy. As I hung up the phone from my conversation

The beautiful altar at the center of the Goddess Temple of Orange County.

with Ava, I remembered Sao's astrological reading in which he told me that one of my soul's missions was to "bring forward the mastery of the mysteries of Venus and Mars."

I thought of the books I was reading about the history of the goddess. Many of them had a tone of anger and hurt toward men, as if their goddess work was really a rejection of the male rather than an attraction toward the feminine. The authors seemed bitter and sarcastic and not loving (even though love is power).

I realized that it's my role to teach that it's not about male-bashing or having the goddess overpower the male—it's about healing our fear of feminine power. We all saw glimpses of this power when our mothers were angry, and it terrified us, making us fear being abandoned, but it also made us angry at her for withdrawing love. We also got mad at ourselves for depending on Mom.

The evening of the Venus Transit, the Goddess Temple was filled to capacity with men and women who felt drawn to goddess and Venus energy. I began speaking about the history of Venus and the goddess.

"Venus is called the morning and the evening star. She dances through the sky as the morning star next to the moon for seven days. Then she disappears for 60 days (it's said she goes to the underworld), and then reappears for seven days next to the moon as the evening star. Then she disappears for another seven days in conjunction with the sun, like a secret romance.

"This cycle was the basis of the goddess Venus's birth and resurrection stories. It's said that when Venus visits the underworld for 60 days, she's freeing the trapped souls of those who have crossed over, and helping them reach the Light.

"Venus has always been revered as a powerful goddess, with the Sumerian culture being our earliest record of her. All cultures have viewed Venus as a sensuous and beautiful goddess who ruled over love and fertility. As the evening star, she's seen as the Goddess of Sensuality and Passion. As the morning star, she's viewed as a the Goddess of Sweet Romance.

"In Sumeria, Venus was called Inanna, 'Queen of Heaven,' or 'The Great Above.' In Babylon, she was called Ishtar; in Syria, her name was Astarte; and in Persia, she was called Anahita. The Romans called her Venus or Veneris, and the Greeks named her

Aphrodite, which means 'foam born.' They believed that Aphrodite was a mixture of water and air, or the feminine and masculine.

"Tonight, Venus is eclipsing the sun. Even though she's much smaller than the masculine sun, Venus is showing her power to shine and make a difference! Like Venus, you're asked to stand up and not shrink from challenges. Venus says that we're all stars like she is. Some may see this event as symbolic of the feminine eclipsing the masculine, while others may say it's a merging of the female and the male energies.

"Venus was banished along with the Mother Goddess in the first through third centuries. She was replaced by a patriarchal, single Father God. Every family needs both a Mother and a Father, so let's invite the banished goddess back now. We need a Mother! A derivation of the word *Mother* is *matter*. When we lose awareness of the Mother, we become materialistic to compensate."

We then all held glasses of water, which we infused with our intentions, and then drank together.

Venus in Las Vegas

The next day, Steven and I flew to Las Vegas to speak at Hay House's I Can Do It® expo. Hay House put up all the speakers at the Venetian Hotel, which featured painted cherubs flying across ceiling murals, and a faux Venetian canal running through its indoor shopping mall.

While falling asleep at the hotel, I realized that *Venice* is a derivation of Venus, and has an association with water (it's a city on the water). The Venus goddess Aphrodite was born from the ocean, so the water and Venus connection was obviously ancient. I thought of the medical term "Venus insufficiency," a description of varicose veins. Venus was deeply imbedded into our lives in some subtle ways!

The next afternoon was my first time teaching about angels since our trip to Lourdes. During this workshop, as I'd noticed while teaching about Venus at the Goddess Temple, I could tell the difference in my teaching style, and knew that I'd been transformed by the Lourdes healing energy. Gone was my sarcastic edge. I was centered in love—Mother love. I felt more patient and understanding of people, and sensed that my inner left-brained businesswoman fears had left (or at least, had stopped controlling me).

I taught a class to about 600 people on the topic of archangels and ascended masters. I discussed eight goddesses, plus Thoth, Hermes, Merlin, and Ganesh and several of the archangels, especially Michael. Then we dimmed the lights and put on music, and I invoked each one with an affirmation:

> *"We now call upon Quan Yin, the Buddhist goddess of compassion. Let us affirm, 'It is safe for me to forgive myself. It is safe for me to forgive others.'*
>
> *"We now invoke Kali, the Hindu goddess of beginnings and endings, and we affirm, 'It is safe for me to be powerful. My power helps others.'*
>
> *"We next call upon Lakshmi, the Hindu goddess who helps us manifest our material needs. Let us affirm, 'It is safe for me to receive. I now receive good graciously into my life.'*
>
> *"Now let us invite Brigit, the Celtic goddess of light and healing. And together let us affirm, 'It is safe for my light to shine brightly.'*
>
> *"And we invoke Aphrodite, the Grecian love goddess. Our affirmation is: 'It is safe for me to be loved. I am lovable right now.'"*

The next day, a woman stopped me to tell me that she'd had an odd experience following my workshop. She said that during the seminar she'd been really open and had invited all of the beings to help her. That night she saw swirling, dancing lights and she felt that they were beings pulling lower energies out of her. "Like an exorcism," she said. "Is this normal?"

I asked, "Did you seeing anything else besides these lights?"

"No."

"Did you feel any negativity?"

"No, it was just very intense."

"But it was a loving energy, right?"

"Oh yes!"

"Well, you had an angel experience! You were visited by the archangels and ascended masters, just as we requested during the workshop. They were healing and helping you."

"Oh, I wish I'd known that so I could have enjoyed it more."

That afternoon I taught another class called "Indigo, Crystal, and Rainbow Children," and Hay House recorded it live for a CD of the same title. The engineer asked everyone in the audience to be as quiet as possible during the workshop so the recording wouldn't have extra noise. Well, the audience took this request to the extreme, and you'd hardly know anyone was there during the entire talk! No one coughed or even wiggled, and no cell phones rang.

Even a small boy named Gabriel in the audience remained still and quiet for the talk. His parents brought the five-year-old to meet me after the workshop. I told him about the large angel wings I saw extending from his shoulder blades, and he began clapping and jumping up and down with excitement.

His mother explained that Gabriel always spoke of his angel wings to her, complaining that as hard as he tried, he still couldn't fly even though he knew he *could*. Gabriel told me about his guardian angel named Crystal, and my heart melted with love for this young Source-erer who so openly talked about his angelic roots and guardians.

Programming Water

Back home the next evening, Shannon Kennedy was giving me a massage. She told me that she'd been receiving messages from Sri Dhanvantari, the original teacher of Ayurveda; however, she couldn't understand what he was trying to say. She asked whether I could talk with him for her. I immediately saw a large man who spoke about very high-level concepts regarding science and medicine in a foreign language. Although I could see and hear him perfectly, I worried whether I could understand him. Shannon said, "Yes, that's him! He's a very brilliant physician who speaks in Sanskrit."

Then, mercifully, he began speaking to me through mental pictures (the universal language). First he showed me a glass container of amber-colored oil. Shannon became excited and explained that all pictures of this man show him holding that vial of oil.

Sri Dhanvantari then showed me sacred geometry and light above the oil and said that we can and should program our healing and essential oil with prayers, light, and intention. He conveyed to me that every liquid we use ought to be programmed with prayer and intentions, including eyedrops, beverages, lotion, food, and shampoo.

He told Shannon through me that she'd been selected to work with him to heal people, and she was his apprentice. He made it clear that he wasn't helping her—she was helping him! We kept talking, and she understood. Then Sri Dhanvantari told her to allow him to channel his healing energy into a tightened muscle in my neck. His energy through Shannon was so powerful that my muscles began to heat up and relax. The pain I'd been feeling left immediately.

I later researched Sri Dhanvantari and found paintings of him that looked similar to how I'd seen him in the spirit world. The paintings did portray him a bit younger and thinner than he looks on the Other Side, undoubtedly out of respect for his legacy, but his paintings do indeed show him holding amber urns and vials.

More Messages

Every day I received messages and signs about water. Either someone would tell me about a healing well, or the angels would talk to me about working with the element of water. When we gave a workshop at the Omega Center in upstate New York the weekend after I spoke with Sri Dhanvantari, a nurse began telling me about the underwater births she specialized in performing. She said that the benefits are shorter labors, a much calmer baby (the infant smiles instead of cries at birth!), and fewer drugs given to the mother.

A few hours later, I led an angel workshop through a channeling exercise in which we contacted Archangel Michael and asked him the question: "What do I need to release to be fully on my path and purpose?"

As soon as I uttered this question to the class, I heard Michael in my right ear, *"Salt. It absorbs water from your cells"* and *"Diuretics—they are water robbers. Drink more water, fluids of any sort. Hydrate, hydrate, hydrate!"*

That night I woke up in the wee hours to hear Michael say, *"Trans-fatty acids lead to tiredness because they make the system [body] sluggish. Trans-fatty acids are difficult to digest, so the energy must be funneled toward digestion instead of other areas."*

As Steven and I drove to the airport the next day, we momentarily worried whether we'd catch our flight on time. From a human standpoint, it appeared that we'd be late and would miss our plane. Since it was the last flight from the East to the West Coast that evening, we'd have to find a hotel. Well, that wasn't an acceptable solution, so we decided to manifest what we desired.

My husband and I used our knowledge of manifestation to lovingly affirm that we'd arrive at the airport exactly at the right time. We stated aloud to each other that we'd easily board our airplane and have our luggage checked in, in plenty of time to travel.

I'd been reading books about alchemy and hermetics, and I'd discovered that in ancient times, alchemists labored to turn base metal (such as lead) into precious metals (like gold). I thought how I much preferred the alchemy of attracting gold and golden situations, instead of trying to create them. As we pulled up to the airport with plenty of time to spare, I felt grateful that Steven and I had used our Source-ery powers.

On the plane, I opened Franz Bardon's classic book, *Initiation into Hermetics.* I smiled as I read Bardon's suggestions from 1956 to infuse wishes into the air and then breathe them in as a means of manifestation. He also advises infusing wishes into water and food and holding the intention of merging with the wish while drinking or eating.

I closed my eyes and smiled as the plane reached cruising altitude. I'd been feeling so happy and filled with love since the Venus transit—and many others had told me the same thing. Venus as a warrior goddess had disarmed us with the most powerful weapon of all: opening our hearts to love. You see, when you're in love, you look for similarities with your beloved. Since the root of all conflict is seeing differences between yourself and another, love truly seems to be the key to eliminating conflict.

Amma, Mother Goddess

Sometimes called "The Hugging Saint," Amma (which means "Ma" or "Mother" in Sanskrit) travels from India to heal people with her hugs. Amma only sleeps two hours a night and gives tirelessly to charities and people who need her. She embraces people into the wee hours, and it's estimated that this dear woman has hugged more than 21 million people around the world.

Steven and I were planning to meet with her in Oakland, but I'd been ambivalent about going to the retreat because we'd been traveling so much. The thought of another plane, hotel room, and rental car felt painful. As we arrived at the Orange County airport to fly to Northern California, I was looking for an excuse to cancel and go home.

I really wanted to see Amma; I just didn't want to go through the hassle of getting there. As soon as I got in touch with this ambivalence, I said to Steven, "Let's talk about this." We sat down, and I explained my feelings. Then I remembered the angels' words: *"When you have to make a decision between two directions, take the path that brings you closer to your life's mission."*

Clearly, the decision bringing me closer to my mission was to see Amma. As we flew into Oakland, an internal message said, *"Go to the bathroom right now!"* as if I were being pushed.

Just as I entered the bathroom, the pilot turned on the "Return to Seat" sign, since we were about to descend. I thought of how often my good timing came from following inner nudges to "Go here now" without hesitation. For instance, by obeying such inner guidance, I'd been able to meet and receive blessings from the Dalai Lama.

Steven and I drove to Amma's center in a charming rural area surrounded by horse farms, birch trees, and duck ponds. We drove along the bumpy dirt road leading to several older buildings at her center and saw hundreds of people in flowy, white-gauze clothing.

Staff members asked if we'd ever seen Amma before, and we said no. Because it was our first time, they stuck fluorescent, round orange stickers on our shirts. Then we were escorted to the front of the *darshan* (blessing) line, where we sat on pillows with other people who were also new to the experience. We were given tissues to wipe off makeup and oil from our faces so that we wouldn't stain Amma's white sari. After an orientation talk, we all stood. Steven and I took our cues from the more experienced audience members and joined them in chanting Sanskrit words meaning "I bow to the Universal Mother."

Everyone moved aside so that an aisle was created down the center of the room. We all looked back as if we were at a wedding awaiting the bride. As Amma walked in, my heart swelled with love for the petite, broad-smiling woman walking past us. Then she sat down on the stage, and we all sat back down.

An English-speaking emcee explained that Amma wants to see men and women work together, and would like men to recognize the power of women. As he lectured about ideal spiritual relationships, Amma sat with her eyes closed, rocking herself and meditating. Her aura was bright green; and she had Gandhi, Krishna, Ganesh, and Babaji with her.

I closed my eyes and looked at Amma psychically. I was shown that she was connected to *very* high dimensions—and many of them. I also saw that she was using most of her parallel lifetimes simultaneously for her mission of healing with love. And just as I'd seen in the Dalai Lama, her route to enlightenment had been through meditation and selfless service.

I thought about the power of meditation, as demonstrated in both Amma and the Dalai Lama's blissful peacefulness. I heard the angels whisper in my ear, *"Meditation gives birth to the purpose that lies in gestation for most people. Even ten minutes a day devoted to cleansing the mind through meditation will take you further than any book or lecture."*

I looked at the violet wristband everyone wore at the retreat, which was printed with words from Amma: "The childlike innocence deep within you is God."

As I scanned Amma's chakras, I saw that her solar plexus was huge, as was her throat chakra. The others were quite small except for her heart chakra, which was so big that it created an outer aura of emerald green. When I see healers, they always have emerald-green auras. Seeing Amma helped me realize that healers' large heart chakras and their love create that emerald aura.

The emcee said that Amma accepts us as we are, and she's like "living love," which doesn't force anyone to change. He explained that because she's so accepting and nonjudgmental, everyone feels comfortable in her presence.

Then it was Amma's turn to speak, and a low microphone stand was placed in front of her so that she could remain in a lotus position. She spoke through a translator and said, "I bow down in front of my children, who are embodiments of pure love." Amma had an earnest expression, a throaty deep voice, and a down-to-earth demeanor. If you met her on the street, you would never have guessed that she's regarded as a living saint. Although I couldn't understand anything she said until her words were translated into English, I felt as if a loving and knowing mother was speaking to me.

She said through the translator, "Eighty percent of diseases are caused by tension, and we must stop worrying or brooding over what we think are problems. You can hold a big cup of coffee for five minutes without pain, but if you hold it all day, the burden becomes increasingly heavier, even though that cup weighs the same. Prayer is the way to unburden ourselves. Prayer is gold—it brings everything we want to us.

"Love is the only thing that can help humanity, for it knows no race, religion, or gender. Where there is division, there can be no unity. Few are willing to explore the world within themselves, choosing instead to study externals. We decorate our homes with beautiful pictures of Mother Nature, yet we pollute her. We need to beautify our minds, and to do this, we need to declare war without bloodshed on negativity. Everyone complains that there isn't enough time and 'I'm so busy'; even little kids are in a hurry. People don't complete tasks."

She described fragmented attention by presenting an example of a man about to wash his car. First he noticed the mail, then got distracted by a dirty glass and unwatered plants. Even though he was busy all day, his car remained unwashed and nothing was fully accomplished. "Many people think of hundreds of things that they need to do, but nothing gets done. What's needed is a total focus on the present moment, instead of the tension that comes from worrying about the future."

Amma then discussed how to heal our relationships. "Understanding another person's mind is important before reacting to that person; otherwise, we'll be overwhelmed with negative reactions toward others. Harboring hatred toward someone is like swallowing poison and expecting the enemy to die. Anger is like holding a knife that's sharpened on both ends, and it cuts whoever holds it.

"Love is the total medicine that treats the disease of the ego. God is the pure consciousness, which dwells within everything and everyone. It's not always easy to love everyone equally, but we should at least try not to be angry with others. Love is our permanent nature, so it isn't an emotion, because emotions change and switch. Love is always there.

"Love is Mother Nature. Love is all-pervasive. Ego imprisons love, and we should pray for love to be let out of its prison. Don't waste your time on trivia. We should set a timetable and stick to it. We need to put necessary effort in that direction. This timetable should be set up to help us break our old negative patterns and to help us move forward in life.

"How to focus? It's like when shopping, narrowing your attention to your intended item. In the same way, when meditating, you must focus on your intentions and not be distracted by unneeded or unwanted thoughts."

After her talk, Amma and several others sang devotional songs. Amma sat and rocked, throwing her arms as if casting light and blessings toward us. I marveled at her vitality, especially since she was due to teach a meditation class at 11 P.M. that night.

Amma led us through a meditation of chanting "Om" (the sound of Universal creation) repeatedly. During the chant, I held the intention of purifying my heart. A voice, perhaps Amma's, whispered in my ear, *"It's not your heart, but your mind, that needs purifying. To purify your heart, you must purify your mind and learn to discipline your thoughts."*

After the chanting began, the emcee announced that it was time for Amma to begin embracing those who came to her for hugs. Amma would begin with hugging the newcomers. Steven and I were fourth in line. We knelt, awaiting our turn. First, she hugged Steven.

My face was then put into her bosom by a temple worker, and Amma held me and whispered words in my ear. Although she spoke in Malayalam, her words sounded like a soothing mother: "Hush, stop crying, worrying, and fussing. There, there. Everything's going to be all right." Amma's hug, her voice, and her energy were completely reassuring, nurturing, and mothering. She then rocked Steven and me in her bosom as a couple, and looked me in the eye before and after. She was amazingly present.

Rock On, Goddess

The next night, Steven and I went to see another living "goddess" with an entirely different style and energy: Stevie Nicks. We went to see her band, Fleetwood Mac, play at the Verizon Wireless Amphitheater in Irvine, California, on a perfect summer evening. Steven stepped into his power by somehow orchestrating a way for us to stand in front of the stage, directly in front of Stevie! I had my arms on the stage and was three feet from her the entire concert.

From the moment she appeared in front of the audience, Stevie was the epitome of a goddess. She stood in her power, expressed herself honestly from her deepest truth (which we all relate to), and she was totally passionate. When she sang "Rhiannon," about the Welsh moon goddess, the entire audience sang along. *How alike Amma and Stevie are!* I thought, having seen them two days apart. Both were beautifully radiant with purpose and passion.

How interesting that we sat for three hours to see Amma, and stood for three hours to see Stevie. Black-haired and blonde-haired living goddesses in one weekend!

Both women are reminders that you can be feminine, beautiful, *and* powerful.

✳ ✳ ✳ ✳ ✳ ✳

Chapter 20

ATLANTIS THERAPY

The next day I stood before my workshop audience and led them through an Atlantean past-life regression. The people of Atlantis were part of a golden age of great spiritual and religious freedom. The era following the demise of Atlantis is filled with accounts of religious persecution. The Sumerians, Babylonians, Egyptians, Jews, and Christians had all been religious persecutors—as well as victims—throughout history.

The pagans had especially suffered due to their beliefs in nature spirits. The word *pagan,* as mentioned earlier, means "country dweller." Yet persecutors created an atmosphere of terror in a marketing campaign to equate paganism with devil worship.

Before then, temples were built to honor Asherah, Isis, Sophia, and other names for the Creator Goddess. It was just assumed that, since women give birth to babies, the Creator was feminine or consisted of a father *and* a mother. Statues of these deities surrounded the temples built in the Creator Goddess's honor. As monotheism (the belief in a solo male God) took hold, these statues were smashed.

In later years, the Catholic church led a crusade to prosecute and execute known pagans for the crime of heresy. As reward for identifying and slaying them, crusaders received part of the land owned by the deceased pagans. Some crusaders were even canonized for their deeds.

My work in teaching clairvoyance classes taught me that many people hold deep-seated memories of these crusades. They fear being killed for reawakening their clairvoyance, just as they were slain for their spiritual gifts in previous lifetimes.

I discovered that if I regressed my students back to their lifetime in Atlantis, they could shed the fear and pain of the crusades. Atlantis provided a cleansing and safe environment, and just by reexperiencing it, my students could open their third eyes without fear of persecution. Whenever my workshop schedule allowed it, I took audiences through this process to help them heal from long-held fears.

Atlantis Past-Life Meditation

I took an advanced class of Angel Therapy Practitioners through an Atlantean past-life regression:

"Let's begin by getting comfortable in your chair, or even lying down if you prefer. Please take some deep breaths, inhaling deeply and then exhaling completely.

"Now allow yourself to see a dolphin. This is your personal dolphin guide, who will take you on your journey back to your life in Atlantis. When you feel ready, please climb onto the dolphin for this journey.

"A big, bright rainbow has just appeared in front of you. Please choose one of the colors of the rainbow rays, as a pathway for you and your dolphin to travel upon. You and your dolphin are now gliding up the rainbow toward the top of the arc.

"As you glide downward toward the vast blue ocean, you're entering the time of Atlantis. You are now in Atlantis. Please look at your feet and notice whether they've changed in any way. Notice your surroundings and who's around you. Notice where you are and what's going on.

"If you haven't already done so, please transport yourself to a Healing Temple. Notice the details of the temple: Who's in there with you? What are they doing? What are *you* doing? Spend as much time in this temple as you'd like.

"When you're ready, please go to a place in Atlantis that was significant for you during your lifetime there. What do you see?

Who's with you? Do you notice any crystals around you?

"When you feel ready, please return with your dolphin to the rainbow. Choose a color to ride along as you slowly and gently return to your present life. You can bring all your knowledge from Atlantis along with you, and you can return to Atlantis anytime you like. Your dolphin will stay with you to assist, heal, and love you."

As the class returned their awareness to the present day, many were in tears, sobbing because they missed the great love they'd felt in Atlantis.

After we'd processed the grief of leaving the "lost continent," I next asked the class members to channel a message from Hermes, the great Atlantean High Priest and spiritual leader. (Hermes left Atlantis before its downfall and went to Egypt, where he was known as Thoth, and to England where he was called Merlin.)

I asked Hermes to write a message through each student as part of the process called "automatic writing." This involves using a pen and paper, or a computer, and calling upon a being in the spirit world. You can think the thought, *Please come to me* directed to a specific being, such as your guardian angel, an archangel, a departed loved one, or an ascended master such as Jesus or Moses. It's best to ask Archangel Michael to stand by during automatic-writing sessions, as he'll ensure the authenticity of the person channeling through you.

Next, ask the spiritual being a question either aloud or silently (they hear your thoughts). Then write any impressions you receive, such as physical or emotional feelings, visions in your mind's eye, words you hear, or thoughts.

Write the words even if you're wondering whether you're imagining the message. The ego fights against our receiving spiritual guidance because it wants us to stay afraid and dependent. The ego's chief tactic is to tell us that we're just making up the Divine guidance we receive. You can always ask the spiritual being, "How do I know I'm not just making you up?" as a way to convince yourself of its genuineness. The answer you'll receive will help you to believe.

I then suggested that class members ask Hermes, "What do I need to know about my life in Atlantis to help me now?" I participated, and asked him this question as well.

He answered, *"There was a concoction you made and drank based upon an herbal variety of chocolate, but much more pure than the variety you currently offer. The cravings for chocolate are the cravings for Atlantis, as well as an earthly desire for the medicinal effects of pure chocolate, unadulterated by sugar, preservatives, and other substances. You have conquered your earthly cravings by substituting an etheric version of chocolate, which Raphael brought to you, to continually feed you on the etheric plane."*

After I received this channeling, Hermes mentioned to me that his name was a play on words. He said, *"My name is actually: He's Mer."* Hermes had a mer-connection to Atlantis, and transported himself away from the flooded continent with his mer-abilities.

Remembering Atlantis

I asked the class (as well as those who listened to this meditation on my two-CD set *Angel Medicine)* to write about their memories of Atlantis. The majority felt blissful during their Atlantean past-life regressions.

As one woman described: "As I looked around this amazing place, I felt real peace. Every cell of my being was at one with each other, at one with all. I felt so relaxed, secure, and alive—truly alive—like never before. I felt that I was home!"

All of the papers on past-life Atlantean memories described similar scenarios:

- People were dressed in long white robes, gowns, or tunics with golden ropes as belts.

- Men and women wore their hair long.

- People had very large feet with webs. Sometimes the feet were finned, especially when the person was swimming in the ocean.

- People could breathe while swimming underwater by pulling oxygen out of the water in their mouths.

- Dolphins co-existed along with people.

- Some people reported that they shape-shifted into mermaids, mermen, or dolphins whenever they entered the water.

- Pools and waterways ran through towns and often within healing temples. There were underground water tunnels that people and dolphins used to transport themselves.

- Buildings were made of marble and crystal, with columns and pillars inside most buildings. Some structures were round, and others were pyramid-shaped.

- There was a Shangri-La atmosphere, with waterfalls and beautiful trees and flowers.

Celtic Water Goddesses

Steven and I drove to Malibu to attend a workshop on Celtic shamanism given by Tom Cowan, the author of *Shamanism as a Spiritual Practice for Everyday Life,* who holds a doctorate in history. The workshop was being held at an oceanfront home with a lovely, large yard that was filled with wildflowers. Neither Steven nor I had ever seen a house on the ocean with such a yard before. All the homes on the beach we'd seen were on small lots without any flowers, trees, or lawn. This was what we'd been looking for! We asked the woman who lived there about the place.

The woman explained that she and her husband had always wanted to live on the oceanfront, in a home with a yard. They'd said affirmations and prayers to manifest such a house since they didn't have much money. Well, in the meantime they met and befriended an elderly man. Within a few years, the man had moved out of the place and into a retirement facility, and he asked the couple to live in his home—the one on the beach with the spectacular yard—for a very low monthly rent. They'd manifested the house of their dreams without having to spend a lot of money!

Steven and I looked at each other upon hearing this story. If *they* could manifest a beautiful oceanfront home with a gorgeous lawn and flowers for very little money, so could we!

We proceeded to the workshop, where Tom began by invoking the Celtic goddess Dana (pronounced *Don-YAH*).

"Dana is often called 'The Waters from Heaven,'" he said, "and many rivers are named for her, including the Danube, Dnieper, Dniester, and the Don. Sacred wells and rivers are considered entryways to the Mother, and Dana was a Mother Creator Goddess.

"It was a Celtic tradition to gather water for healing at the first light of dawn. Healers would take this water to a 'Bulaun,' a rock with a natural hole in it that collects rainwater. That water is considered especially powerful for healing. You can also rub two stones over water to bring the power of the earth into the water for healing."

Tom then invoked the Celtic goddess Brigit. He said, "In the name of Brigit, the ancient Celts held a water-blessing ceremony." He led us through the ceremony, using water that had been in the middle of the workshop circle. He paired us up and had us sprinkle water onto our partner. "First, put water on the feet so that their path will be true. Next, bless their hands with the water so their work will be true. Then, bless their head with water so their thoughts will be true."

My hands tingled, and I felt the hundreds of chakras that are in everyone's hands sparkling cleanly and brightly. While most people are familiar with the major chakras in the body, I'd learned from the angels and also from pranic healing and other Eastern healing classes that the entire body is filled with chakras. The hands have the highest concentrated number of them, so they're the most sensitive to receiving and sending energy. I use my hand chakras during in-person readings by sweeping my hands a few inches above my client's head and shoulders. The hand chakras detect "hot spots" where angels and spirit guides are hovering nearby. These chakras also translate energy into mental pictures that you can see in your mind's eye as you're performing the hand scan.

The hand chakras also detect energy within a room or an object, just by slowly waving the hands and noticing impressions that come to you. For instance, if you need to find a parking space, hold your hand out and you'll receive the energy of the empty space through its chakras. You can also put your hands out and ask for the location of a missing item. The hand chakras will detect anything or anyone you put your intentions upon.

You can also sweep away negative energy with your hands in a motion I call the "Source-eress's Sweep." Anytime you say (or someone else says) a negative word, or if you feel negativity in a room, push it away by sweeping your hand in a smooth motion from just above your head. Push away the energy with a fluid sweep of your hand, making a U shape from just above your head using the back of your hand, and then sweep up the U angle until your palm faces away from you.

During our lunch break, Steven and I drove to a nearby salad bar. As we sat outside eating, Steven discussed the idea for his new book. He was thinking of composing an e-mail to our publisher, Hay House. I had a strong inner knowing that he should pitch this new book in person and not by e-mail, and I told him so.

Just as I said that, a raven flew in front of us. I said, "See?" and Steven shrugged. Just then a second raven flew by. I said, "See?" Steven still shrugged. I said, "Do you want a third raven to convince you?" even though I couldn't see any other ravens anywhere. I said it purely on faith. One second later, a third raven went by. Steven laughed and said, "Very good! That was good!" Steven did end up pitching the book in person, and Hay House said yes.

I'd had so many experiences with ravens that I'd learned to trust their instinctual magical abilities. After all, these birds have long been associated with wizards and alchemists. I'd been surprised to discover that the raven was one of my power animals during Steven's workshop on the topic. I'd always assumed I'd have fluffy, feminine power animals like a dove or a dolphin. I'd known for years that I worked with a black jaguar, and had recently discovered Dino the golden dragon at my side. When I discovered that my third power animal was a raven, I was surprised at first. Then I realized that my trio of animal guides helped me deal with the shadow side of my healing and psychic work. They also protected me during my travels and in my interactions with people.

Manifesting Our Dream Home

Steven and I returned from the Malibu workshop with a renewed commitment to manifesting an oceanfront home. I called April, our real estate agent, and asked her to scour listings for any new homes on the market. She found several, yet each had a problem. Either the home was too expensive, had no yard, was in need of too much renovation, or was out of Laguna Beach.

I realized that I was "pushing" to make the manifestation happen. Anytime we *try to* make something happen, there's an underlying fear that stems from the ego. The fear might be, "What if it won't happen?" or "What if I don't deserve this?" Any fear slows or blocks manifestation.

In ancient times, virgins and animals were ritually sacrificed to please, appease, and bribe the gods. Today, we don't kill virgins or lambs, but do we still hold deep-seated fears that we need to sacrifice something to get what we want. That belief becomes self-fulfilling, and we sacrifice getting enough sleep, exercise, or playtime while struggling to get ahead.

In truth, the universe is all-providing. Matter is made of the same malleable energy as our thoughts and emotions; consequently, we're always manifesting and attracting according to these thoughts and emotions. We can't shut this ability off—what we can do, though, is choose more carefully.

So Steven and I spent time discussing our fears about manifesting a new home. As soon as we faced these fears, they burst like soap bubbles on a summer day. Then, we separately wrote detailed descriptions of the house of our dreams. When we read those lists to each other, we were pleased to find that they matched almost perfectly.

Each morning and night, we held hands and said together, "Thank you, Creator, for our beautiful oceanfront home that we love so much and easily afford." We also looked at the collage we'd made, with photos of beautiful beach houses. We imagined ourselves happily owning a home with similar features.

A week later, April called about a place that had just gone on the market. I instantly felt strongly that this was the one. The price and location were right, and when we arrived to see it, Steven and I were thrilled to find a yard filled with colorful flowers. The interior of the house was ideal, too. That night we signed an offer to purchase it.

※ ※ ※ ※ ※ ※

Chapter 21

LEMURIA AND MERPEOPLE

While our new house was in escrow, Seven and I were invited to speak on a cruise ship along with James Van Praagh, the psychic medium. My husband and I had never been on a cruise before, outside of a brief weekend jaunt from Long Beach, California, to Ensenada, Mexico. But we'd always wanted to visit Tahiti, so we agreed to go.

The ship was elegant, and because it was sailing in shallow reefs between the islands, it was smaller than the massive ocean liners that sail across the oceans.

We ate our dinners with James and his family at a large circular table in the dining room, along with the seminar participants and other people on the cruise. I'd notified the cruise director that I was a vegan, so I was served tofu and vegetables each night.

Ever since visiting Lourdes, I always blessed my food and beverages before consuming them. I visualized Mother Mary inside my water container, and could feel its energy shift. I also found that I could spread prayer energy on my food by waving my right hand above the meal. I saw colorful geometric shapes leave the palm of my hand and enter the food, like butter melting on hot toast.

One evening after our meal, I drew the shapes that came from my hand. They looked like intersecting pyramids, with the Star of David shape inside. I later discovered that they were icosahedrons, the 20-sided Platonic solid associated with the element of Water.

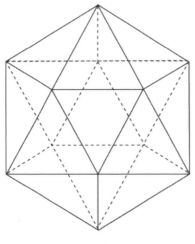

An icosahedron.

Magical Paradise

Bora-Bora had to be the most beautiful place I'd ever visited. The island's mountain peak glowed a surreal shade of green, and its jagged edges looked otherworldly. The island held a distinctly masculine warrior energy, and I heard echoes of ancient chants.

As Steven and I snorkeled around the perfectly transparent turquoise waters, I saw visions of stalagmite clear quartz crystals coming up from the bottom of the sea. The crystals were once there physically, but they'd shifted upward in vibration and were now in the etheric dimensions. I was seeing energetic imprints of the previous physical existence of the crystals below the sea.

The next day, Steven decided to go scuba diving with me. It was his first open-water dive since his Introduction to Scuba Diving certification course, so we went with an instructor named Dominique.

Dominique brought along a loaf of bread in his scuba vest, which certainly made us popular—we were surrounded by dazzling tropical fish of all shapes and sizes! As we swam along underwater, a procession followed us, including a trumpet fish with the longest snout I'd ever seen! I called him "Horsey," and he, along with bright yellow, orange, and blue fish, swam faithfully by our sides.

Just below the boat, I noticed that Steven was breathing from Dominique's "octopus" secondary air supply, and they were ascending to the surface together. When I went up, Steven told me that he'd run out of air just as our dive ended. He made the out-of-air hand signal (which consists of moving your hand across your neck) to Dominique, who then rescued Steven. Given that it was Steven's first open-water dive, he stayed remarkably calm and didn't panic at all.

In addition to the major islands around Tahiti, there are dozens of smaller uninhabited islands called *motus* (pronounced: *MOE-tooz*). Each hour, a small "tender boat" shuttled passengers from our cruise ship to the motus. After our scuba-diving adventure, I was pleasantly surprised when Steven said he wanted to swim there.

The motu off of Bora-Bora looked like a postcard of paradise. Imagine the brightest and clearest turquoise ocean water next to silky white sandy beaches; tall, curvy palm trees; and a dramatic green mountain in the distance.

As I snorkeled, rainbow lights danced and radiated throughout the water. I meditated with my eyes closed, floating with my face underwater while breathing through the snorkel. I felt like a mermaid who'd come home. I asked, "Is this the location of the ancient civilization known as Lemuria?"

Bora-Bora's beaches are like postcards of paradise.

I heard the answer: *"No, Lemuria was on the other side of the world. This was an antediluvian society like Lemuria, though. There were many cultures like Atlantis and Lemuria concurrent with them and over the seven seas."* The voice then repeated the phrase "seven seas" so many times that I thought of the Eurythmics song "Sweet Dreams Are Made of This" and the lyric, "I travel the world and the seven seas."

Antediluvian means "before the great deluge flood described in Genesis and pre-Judaic texts and cultures." The Babylonians' story is identical to Noah's, even to the white dove foretelling the end of the deluge. Scientific evidence shows that a major comet hit the Mediterranean Sea around 3150 B.C., the time of Noah's flood. A previous comet strike in 7640 B.C. may have also besieged the earth.

Lemuria is believed to have sunk in the earliest flood, and Atlantis perished in the second deluge.

Characteristics of Merpeople

As I swam underwater, I received the message that people's different eye colors related to the element they were associated with. People with brown eyes had strong connections with the earth and its spirituality, such as animals, birds, trees, crystals, plants, and fairies. Those with blue eyes were associated with the air element, so they easily attuned to angels and ETs. People with yellow tinges in their brown eyes were connected to the fire element and beings of fire, such as Archangel Michael, the goddess Brigit, and Pele. Those with green eyes were associated with water, and so could easily connect with fish, water mammals, seabirds, and mermaids.

The information surprised me, even as it intuitively resonated as the truth. I wondered why I was given such information. I'd written the book *Earth Angels* about the various realms that lightworkers originated from, based upon similar information I'd received. Those who've read the book usually report that it helps them understand themselves better. They tell me that it's a relief to know the reasons for their behaviors, personality, likes, and dislikes.

Ever since I'd written about these realms (which include incarnated angels, incarnated elementals, wise ones, merpeople, star people, and walk-ins), I'd asked my students at my three- and six-day psychic-development classes to break into groups according to their realms. This allowed me to study these realms even more closely.

Since the publication of *Earth Angels*, I discovered that incarnated leprechauns are actually half-elemental and half-wise ones. They are, after all, the wise Tuatha Dé Dannan who escaped the Gaelic invasion of Ireland by shape-shifting into leprechauns. I'd also found that merangels are one-half angel and one-half elemental. So, merangels have characteristics of both realms.

I'd noticed that merpeople of all races share similar characteristics: They have auburn-red tones in their blonde, brunette, or black hair. They all have green in their eyes, either as pure green, hazel brown with green, or blue with green. I decided to create a survey to find whether these patterns held true in larger samples.

I placed a notice in my monthly newsletter, asking those who resonated with the definition of merpeople to please complete my survey. I asked participants to identify whether they thought they were definitely a merperson, probably a merperson, or undecided. I selected only the surveys of those who said they were definitely a merperson. Most based this opinion on the fact that they matched my descriptions, they *had* to live near water, they'd identified with mermaids or mermen since childhood, had frequent dreams about mermaids, and so on.

Of all the measures on the survey, the significant factors were :

- 82% had a natural red tint or highlights in their hair
- 82% preferred to wear their hair long (89% of just the females surveyed)
- 79% had naturally curly or wavy hair
- 69% had green in their eyes
- 85% reported being frequently or constantly thirsty for water
- 80% said they felt cold often, even in warm weather

The 82 percent of red- and auburn-haired respondents eclipses the estimated 2 to 10 percent of people with naturally red or auburn hair in the general population. Apparently, red hair is a genetic anomaly. At one time, red-haired women were accused of witchcraft. In the 16th and 17th centuries, red-headed European women were put to death during the witch-hunting crusades. Could they have been merpeople who retained their magical abilities and knowledge? Perhaps they were mer-acle workers!

Many of the mer-survey participants described their measures to stay healthy and warm, including taking frequent sea-salt baths, eating kelp or seaweed-based foods, taking frequent vacations in warm tropical locales, and avoiding cold-weather climates.

One woman wrote: "Since I was three years old, I knew how to swim without any lessons. I have to wrap my feet in wet towels every night to avoid pain. I also have scales on my legs that no cream or dermatologist has been able to cure. I move in the water like a mermaid and once set a world record for my butterfly stroke, even though I'd never received any formal training."

※ ◉ ※

The next day our cruise ship pulled into the bay of Mooréa, and I marveled at the contrast between the islands. Bora-Bora had a distinctly male-warrior energy, and I'd heard the etheric voice of deep, throaty male chants during our entire stay on that island.

Now, as we approached Mooréa, I heard a choir of feminine, angelic voices. They were sweet and pure, with overtones of fairy laughter. I'd learned that Bora-Bora natives hadn't been able to raise crops or cattle on their land, so they'd become warlike to violently steal food from the inhabitants of other islands.

Mooréa, in contrast, is called "The Island of Golden-Haired Fairies" because of reported sightings of blonde fairies by island natives. I was also intrigued because Mooréa sounded a lot like Le Mooréa, or Lemuria.

So, as we pulled up to the island, I expected to see Celtic fairies, but I immediately saw that they weren't traditional fairies. They were Menehunes, who have golden-red hair and dark skin and eyes. This made perfect sense, as the Hawaiian islands are also filled with Menehunes, and Hawaii shares Pacific-Asian roots with Tahiti.

Before we'd arrived in Mooréa, I'd had psychic visions of a Polynesian woman with long silky hair whose face was turned upward toward the sunshine. As we pulled up to Mooréa, the first thing I saw was a mountain peak in a perfect silhouetted shape of the woman of my visions. The smooth mountains of Moorea were so feminine in contrast to the sharp, craggy landscape of Bora-Bora.

Next, I saw a large mountain in the exact shape of a castle. It reminded me of the crystal castles I'd seen in Atlantis and Lemuria during my past-life journeys. Everyone on the deck of our ship immediately noticed the castle-shaped mountain. Many gasped and spontaneously said the same thing: "It's a crystal castle!" Even though the "castle" was covered with greenery, you could see and feel its crystal energy.

The similarity between the castles of Atlantis, Lemuria, and Moorea was one more indication that Mooréa was concurrent with, and probably influenced by, the two ancient civilizations.

The next day, Steven and I went on a nature hike with other passengers, led by an archaeologist/ historian named Mark Eddowes. As we started off on the jungle trails, I invoked an etheric covering of fine

The Crystal Castle on the Island of Mooréa.

purple netting over everyone in our group to protect us from mosquitoes and other stinging insects. I also asked unicorns to guide our walk over the rocky and hilly terrain. We weren't bothered once by insects, and we walked with a sure-footed and steady gait.

Our guide, Mark, was the author of a book called *Mooréa of the Society Islands.* He'd adopted the work of his professor, who'd studied Tahitian archaeological sites since the 1950s. Mark was knowledgeable about the esoteric and spiritual history of the islands, as well as more mainstream historical facts.

I mentioned the Menehune to Mark, and he immediately confirmed that Mooréa was inhabited by Menehune elementals, just like Hawaii. Seeing my interest in spirituality and metaphysics, Mark began teaching our group about Tahitian spirituality.

The Tahitians accord women equal status with men, Mark explained. So, they have goddesses, queens, and high-ranking women. "Women have sacred magic in their bodies, while men do not, according to the Tahitians," Mark said. "So men have to build temples in order to commune with their ancestors, so they can draw upon the spiritual power, or *mana,* of their ancestors. Women are considered to have their own natural mana, so they don't need to get it from ancestors." He then told us that the *Tacuras* are female shamans who heal with the help of spirits, while male shamans tend to use plant spirit medicine.

Life began from a male and a female Creator, according to ancient Tahitian spiritual beliefs. The male Creator is Ta'aroa, and he is responsible for creating physicality. The female creator is Atea, and she animates physical life with wisdom and enlightenment. The male is the body, and the female the soul.

Hina (pronounced *HEEN-ah*) is a major goddess within Tahitian spirituality. She's a moon and fertility goddess who was considered so beautiful that no one could look at her. Hina's parents were the moon and the sun, and when Hina returned to the moon one day, she looked down upon the Tahitians and felt pity for their struggles. So she took some pieces of the moon and threw them upon the earth, where they grew into banyan trees. Today, the pieces Hina threw are the dark spots and craters in the moon, and the Tahitians use banyan trees to create tapa cloth.

Crystals are dominant features in the healing lore of Atlantis and Lemuria, and I'd seen many visions of crystals underwater while swimming in the Tahitian islands. So my ears perked up when Mark began discussing the topic. He said that people regularly find clear quartz crystal fragments in the Mooréan valleys. "Someone even found a raw rose quartz crystal in the lagoon of the ocean here in Mooréa," Mark recalled. He pulled me aside and mentioned that he'd heard about three major crystals that balanced the earth within the triangle of islands of Mooréa, Kauai, and Easter Island.

"What about Lemuria?" I asked.

"Some islands were mapped here in the Marquesas Islands in the 1600s, which weren't here in the 1700s during Captain Cook's journey. Many of the islands here have sunk or are sinking," Mark replied.

Then he took me aside and, almost in a whisper, told me about two types of island inhabitants: The first were the Mokoroa—most of them female—who live within the inner earth. This reminded me of the people I'd learned about in Greece who were supposed to be Atlanteans but who had moved their civilization within the earth.

"There's also the Tamahu people," Mark continued. "They had white skin, reddish-blond hair, and green-hazel eyes, and they were here well before the European settlers. These people were held as beings of great beauty, and their hair was precious and full of sacred mana, and often made into ornaments."

I stopped walking and asked Mark to repeat himself. The red hair and green eyes—those were merpeople traits! I told Mark about my research and surveys about merpeople, and he listened with rapt attention. I was grateful that another scientist had an open mind about the possibility that we once lived like the dolphins.

Mark's words made me think of Atlantis's merperson connection. As Atlantis was sinking, some people escaped by shape-shifting into dolphins. They swam to Africa, South America, or Mexico, where their Atlantean knowledge of pyramid-building, healing, and such formed the basis for the Egyptian, Mayan, and Atztec cultures. Ancient legend says that Apollo was in dolphin form when he arrived in Greece. When he shape-shifted back into his human form, a shrine called Delphi was built in his honor (*Delphi* basically means "dolphin" in Greek). Many deities were Atlantean leaders, including Athena, Apollo, Thoth, Metatron, and Merlin.

The Tahitians also believed in merpeople, Mark said. "*Meherio* is the Tahitian version of merpeople, who are often seen as mermaids. They are positive beings who protect those lost at sea. Often they morph into beautiful girls who come onto the land at sunset to seduce young warriors and chiefs. The Meherios talk these men into returning with them in the morning, in secret, back to the sea. The Meherio generally give birth to exceptional beings in the human world, but nearly always after being briefly with the humans, they return to the sea."

Mark also told me about the Tahitian deity, Tinirau, who's half man and half shark. He watches over people who are half shark as well. So the Tahitians believe humans originated from the ocean, and we share a common ancestory with the dolphins, sharks, and other sea creatures. I marveled at how synchronistically this information had come to me.

Over and Under the Water

When the cruise ended, Steven and I rented an over-the-water bungalow on Mooréa. I'd seen photos of these bungalows over the years and had fantasized about how wonderful it would be to jump in the ocean right from your hotel-room balcony. So, the first morning of our visit, I donned my bathing suit, snorkel gear, and fins and did just that from our bungalow. I squirreled a piece of bread into my swimsuit and discovered that the secret to popularity among fish is to bring food! My swim was accompanied by neon-blue, bright-yellow, and striped sergeant fish. I felt like Mama Mermaid, with a trail of hungry fish swimming behind me.

That afternoon we decided to go scuba diving. Steven was a little nervous, considering that he'd run out of air on his first dive. When we arrived at the dive shop, we found a dozen chain-smoking people rapidly speaking French. Although Steven knew some high-school French, their conversations went completely over his head, so communicating through body language, we managed to get our scuba gear and board the correct boat.

Steven's second dive went much better than his first, as he'd learned to check his air gauge at regular intervals. We swam very close to large reef sharks who seemed surprisingly sweet and graceful. I felt in my element swimming freely through the water.

That night Steven and I attended a dinner show called "Tahitian Mamas." The matronly islanders sang with powerful gusto, like a tropical version of gospel singers. One Mama caught my attention because she sang with more abandon and glee than the others. *She really has her heart open,* I thought as I watched her admiringly.

As if she'd heard my thoughts, the Mama walked over to me, grabbed my hand, and led me to the stage. She motioned for me to sit beside her on the edge of the stage. I felt completely enveloped by her motherly energy. I put my arms out, asking for a hug, and she gave me a strong mother-bear embrace that just melted me into her soft, matronly body.

Mama then motioned for me to follow her lead in making a lei wreath. She handed me a large needle and thread and a basket of fragrant plumeria and bougainvillea flowers. I was so happy to be in her presence of simple, pure love. We didn't need to talk with each other; we just shared in joy. As she made a headdress of flowers, Mama belted out a song in perfect harmony with the chorus performing onstage.

I sewed a flower facing the wrong direction, and Mama lovingly laughed and took the lei from me to gently correct my mistake. Her firm strength came from love and a clear sense of direction—she knew herself and didn't question it. *Hers* was true power!

When we were both done sewing, Mama tied the lei and hung it around my neck. She then ceremoniously placed the headdress on my head. Finally, she gave me a big soft hug and kissed me on both cheeks with an abandon that would have embarrassed a self-conscious person.

I walked away feeling totally loved and mothered. What a goddess Mama was! She had nothing to prove, no agenda . . . just the joy of sharing simple pleasures of sewing flowers into a lei and singing with her friends.

On to Australia

The next day Steven and I flew to Sydney for our

Wearing the Tahitian Mama's headdress and lei.

national workshop tour. At my book signings, I kept noticing how many green- and hazel-eyed, auburn-haired people I met who all fit the bill of merpeople. They all reported an obsessive need to be near the ocean or other bodies of water, and said that they frequently felt cold and thirsty. I thought again about the correlation between eye color and element types:

- Green eyes—water element
- Blue eyes—air element
- Brown eyes—earth element
- Yellowish-brown eyes—fire element

As if to confirm this, it seemed that all the blue-eyed people in our group in Sydney wanted to go on the Sydney Harbour Bridge climb, including Wayne Dyer; his girlfriend, Ellen; and Donna (my son Grant's wife). The blue-eyeds apparently don't mind being up in the air! I was not about to climb 440 feet in the air, nor was my hazel-eyed son, Grant.

I asked Rose Rosetree, the author of *The Power of Face Reading,* if she'd noticed any distinguishing characteristics related to people's eye colors. (I didn't tell her about my research to avoid influencing her answer.)

Rose told me that she'd definitely noticed strong personality traits associated with eye colors. She said that blue-eyed people were more geared toward ideas and intellectualism. This fit with the element of air, which is associated with the intellect.

Rose remarked that green-eyed people were more emotional, especially if they also had red hair. This fit with the element of water, which correlates with emotions. She explained that brown-eyed people were down-to-earth, which fit in with the earth element. Rose then told me that people with yellow in their brown eyes were intensely passionate, which fit in with the fire element.

I went for a walk in Hyde Park to think about this information. If we're all from the water originally, why would green- or hazel-eyed people exhibit this trait so strongly?

I let these questions go at the sound of the fountain in the middle of the park. A statue of the Greek deity Apollo and his goddess sister, Artemis, stood in full glory. They were surrounded by magnificent fountains spraying water in an upward arc.

Just behind Artemis stood another monument to a goddess: St. Mary's Cathedral. Its dramatic gothic architecture looked like a

long series of "M's" standing for Mary and Mother. I sat on a bench in front of Artemis, soothed by the sunshine and the water from the fountain above her statue.

As I meditated, I received the answer: *"All human bodies are merbodies, built for*

Honoring two goddesses: Artemis in front of St. Mary's Cathedral in Sydney's Hyde Park.

the water. Everyone is a merperson of one form of another. The green-eyed, auburn-haired people seem to have the most mer-characteristics because they were the last to come out of the water and live upon land. In the meantime, the others were exploring other realms of the vast universe, or upon the great planet Earth."

So those with green in their eyes and red in their hair were like the children who stayed in the swimming pool until closing time.

The Aquatic Ape

That night I dreamed about dolphins. Actually, it seemed more like a dolphin visitation than a dream. I woke up knowing that humans were biologically connected to dolphins, and I felt compelled to research the connection.

The dolphins guided my Internet search of the topic, and within minutes I came across a topic I'd never before heard of called The Aquatic Ape Theory. This theory states that the human body has more similarities to aquatic mammals such as dolphins, seals, and manatees than to primates. Aquatic Ape Theory was first introduced by Sir Alister Hardy, a University of Oxford zoology professor, and then later popularized by Elaine Morgan, a British researcher and author of *The Descent of Woman* (a play on the title of Charles Darwin's primate evolutionary book, *The Descent of Man*). I next purchased and read Hardy's and Morgan's books on the topic.

According to The Aquatic Ape Theory, the human body evolved as our ancestors spent five to six hours daily swimming or wading in the water, finding and eating food and sea vegetables. Hardy and Morgan point out the features that make the human body ideally suited for water climates:

- **Hairlessness.** Humans have "hairless" bodies like other water mammals, so we can swim more aerodynamically. What hair we do have on our bodies grows in the same direction as swimming forward through water currents. Primates and other land-dwelling creatures have fur to protect them from the sun and other elements.

- **Subcutaneous fat.** Only humans and water mammals have a subcutaneous (immediately under the skin) layer of fat, which provides perfect temperature insulation in cold waters. Primates and other land-dwelling animals store fat in membranes and around their internal organs.

- **Protruding female breasts.** Human female breasts are quite similar to female manatees. Protruding breasts are ideal for feeding babies while in the water, providing a way for babies to grasp onto the mother while nursing. Female primates' breasts don't protrude.

- **Weeping.** Only water-dwelling mammals and humans weep tears when they're upset. Scientists believe the tear glands in water-dwellers help balance the salt levels in the body, as well as eliminate waste products secreted during emotional stress. Primates and other land-dwellers only secrete tears to moisturize the eyes or when they're ill, not to express emotion.

- **Nose flaps.** Human nostril muscles are similar to seals, in that we can partially close them to keep out water while swimming.

- **Hair on the head.** The reason why humans still have hair on their heads may lie within clues from the aborigines. Female members of an aboriginal tribe in Patagonia spend a lot of time in the water. If the women carried their babies in their arms while swimming or wading, they'd be thrown off-balance—instead, babies hold on to their mothers' long hair. Elaine Morgan contends that this may be why women's hair tends to grow thicker during pregnancy, and why women rarely go bald. This could also explain why 89 percent of the female merpeople I surveyed prefer to wear their hair long.

- **Webbing.** Humans have webbing between the thumb and index finger, unlike primates. We also have a small

amount of webbing between our fingers, and about
7 percent are born with webbed toes.

- **Swimming.** Primates and land mammals swim with
  their heads above water. Humans and water mammals
  dive and swim underwater.

- **Copulation.** Only water-dwelling mammals mate face-
  to-face. Human and water mammal genitals are located
  on the front of the body. Land-dwellers copulate with
  the male behind the female, mainly because mating in
  trees or on the open ground makes this the most stable
  position. The vagina of most primates and land dwellers
  is situated beneath the tail.

- **Oil.** The millions of sebaceous glands on our face and
  scalp weren't designed to cause teenage angst over acne.
  The chief purpose of body-secreted oil is to provide
  waterproofing.

- **Breathing.** Humans and dolphins can control their
  breathing rate, a feat that allows one to purposely hold
  the breath before diving. The breathing rate of land
  dwellers and primates is automatically controlled, and
  only changes as a reaction and not as a conscious plan.
  In addition, only humans, sea lions, and dugongs (a
  water mammal) have a descended larynx, which keeps
  water out of the lungs while diving.

Hardy and Morgan argue that humans' chief diet was fish
and sea vegetables, which they obtained by diving or wading.
This healthful "smart food" diet helped the human brain grow
significantly and proportionately larger than primates and land
dwellers. Hardy believes that humans first developed tools to
catch fish more efficiently. And because females gathered sea
vegetables and fish while wading in cool waters, they developed
more subcutaneous fat in their lower bodies. (This theory certainly
explains why female merpeople and paintings of mermaids have
hourglass figures.)

The researchers also contend that the human's upright posture is ideal for wading and swimming. One reason why so many people complain of back pain is that the human body is not built for the stress of living on land. In fact, the moment we stand up, our body reacts to the stress by immediately hoarding its inner salt supply.

Elaine Morgan writes:

> It is now generally agreed the man/ape split occurred in Africa between 7 and 5 million years ago, during a period known as the fossil gap. Before it there was an animal which was the common ancestor of human and African apes. After it, there emerged a creature smaller than ourselves, but bearing the unmistakable hallmark of the first shift towards human status: it walked on two legs.
>
> This poses two questions: "Where were the earliest fossils found?" and "Do we know of anything happening in that place at that time that might have caused apes and humans to evolve along separate lines?" The oldest pre-human fossils (including the best known one, "Lucy") are called *australopithecus afarensis* because their bones were discovered in the afar triangle, an area of low lying land near the Red Sea. About 7 million years ago that area was flooded by the sea and became the Sea of Afar.
>
> Part of the ape population living there at the time would have found themselves living in a radically changed habitat. Some may have been marooned on off-shore islands—the present day Danakil Alps were once surrounded by water. Others may have lived in flooded forests, salt marshes, mangrove swamps, lagoons or on the shores of the new sea, and they would all have had to adapt or die.
>
> Aquatic Ape Theory suggests that some of them survived, and began to adapt to their watery environment. Much later, when the Sea of Afar became landlocked and finally evaporated, their descendants returned to the mainland of Africa and began to migrate southwards, following the waterways of the Rift Valley upstream.
>
> There is nothing in the fossil record to invalidate this scenario, and much to sustain it. Lucy's bones were found at Afar lying among crocodile and turtle eggs and crab claws at the edge of a flood plain near what would then have been the coast of Africa.
>
> Other fossils of Australopithecus, dated later, were found further south, almost invariably in the immediate vicinity of ancient lakes and rivers. We now know that the change from the ape into Australopithecus took place in a short space of time, by

evolutionary standards. Such rapid speciation is almost invariably a sign that one population of a species has become isolated by a geographical barrier such as a stretch of water.

I next discovered new research showing how females share common mitochondrial (the part which doesn't change in offspring) DNA that can be traced to one woman who lived about 170,000 years ago. Scientists at U.C. Berkeley named this woman "Mitochondrial Eve," since their studies show that modern females from varied races and cultures all share a common mitochondrial sequence. Further research is confirming this finding, and has pinpointed Mitrochondrial Eve's location to Africa.

The date of Eve's existence places her right after the melting of the Ice Age. Africa's warm climate may have melted the Ice Age's frost there first. Some theorists believe that her tribe waded along the sea, eating fish and sea plants. This watery existence no doubt spurred the need for an aquatic body.

Healing with the Dolphins

My research next led me to a couple in Puna, Hawaii, who conduct underwater births with free dolphins in a bay near Hilo. Paradise Newland was involved with dolphin-assisted birthing in the Red Sea. Her partner, Michael T. Hyson, Ph.D., a neurobiologist, became convinced of the healing power of dolphins when his own neck injury was healed.

Michael recalls, "When I was 12 years old, I compressed the sixth and seventh cervical vertebrae hitting a swimming-pool wall in a dive. When I was 40 and swimming with dolphins in Florida, I heard and felt some loud and tightly focused sonar pulses all over my head and neck that lasted about a second.

"An hour later, the muscles on the left side of my neck relaxed, several places along my back got hot as the blood circulation changed, and then I felt and heard three vertebrae click and move into new positions. When I moved my neck, it was looser, and the grinding sound that had been there since I was 12 was gone.

"After thinking about and studying this for years, I believe we now have at least some idea how the dolphin did this. First, her sonar could put out a peak power near a kilowatt, or about a horsepower. Because of the high frequencies and the four sound sources, this could be focused to under a millimeter. This is enough energy to polish bone.

"Since this happened, I learned that the 'melon,' a lens of oil just under the dolphin's forehead, is piezoelectric, like a quartz crystal. This means that when it's vibrated with sound, it will generate electromagnetic fields. These were measured by Dr. Eldon Byrd and Dean Rawlings. So the dolphins can produce powerful sound and electric fields. There is data on the many effects high-intensity sound and electricity have on our bodies. So, I think that's basically how she healed my neck. These mechanisms can account for many of the healings that are reported.

"Dr. Steven Birch showed that dolphin sounds could change the frequency and power of the brain waves, and by a process called *entrainment,* could release endorphins. Basically, parts of our bodies are piezoelectric. Vibrations of bone and collagen, for example, generate electric currents. The dolphin sounds vibrating the body can cause this. In addition, the sounds can resonate body structures and affect them directly. Medical ultrasound can also change the DNA by activating or turning off different genes. So the dolphins could do the same sort of things with their sounds.

"One of the most dramatic reports is of a child with microcephaly [where the skull plates in a way that will make too small a skull] who improved by being with the dolphins for about a week. It was reported that after being with four dolphins who 'ensonified' the child with sounds for 20 minutes a day, the skull plates were developing normally after about a week. There are similar stories for many different conditions where the dolphins appear able to help."

Entrainment

As I was conducting research on dolphins and merpeople, a graduate of my Australian angel intuitive program named Melinda Jane Maxfield had a remarkable dream. It began with her attending a gathering of graduates of my psychic-development programs. I was teaching my students how to manifest with a specific intention, which is called "entrainment."

In her dream I said, "Through specific intention held toward an object (or person, or event) when placed beside another, it will take on the form of that object, person, or event. It's kind of like shape-shifting."

I demonstrated this by holding a blue ruler next to a plain-colored ruler. I put intention on the plain ruler, and it glowed red just before morphing into the identical color of the blue ruler. She said that I had encouraged the students to practice this technique, and she was amazed at how easy it was.

As Melinda recounted this dream, I recognized it as a true soul-travel experience. I frequently wake up, aware that I either attended or taught advanced classes during the night. Most of the time when I teach during soul travels, the graduates of my psychic-development courses are with me, so what she said made sense.

I'd never heard the term *entrainment* before, yet within one week, both Melinda's dream and my interview with Michael Hyson about dolphins yielded the term! Obviously, my higher self was far wiser than my conscious mind. I found myself in the unusual situation of doing research about something I already knew somewhere in my soul.

Ironically, the definition of the word *entrainment* came to me synchronistically. As I interviewed Michael Hyson and his partner, Paradise Newland, a second time, I remarked how quickly I could swim when I'm with dolphins. "Almost like you're on a bicycle and have caught a draft from a truck driving in front of you," Michael remarked.

"Yes! When I swim with dolphins, the laws of gravity disappear, and I go at lightning speed," I replied.

"That's because of entrainment," Michael and Paradise said simultaneously.

"How interesting you'd use that word . . ." I said.

"Yes, when you swim with dolphins, you become more relaxed." Michael explained that entrainment is when our body rhythms (breath, brain waves, heartbeat, and so on) synchronize with outer rhythms, such as blinking lights, other people's breath or brain-wave rates, or the dolphins' sonars. Our bodies track and match the core frequency and phase of periodic signals, such as rhythmic sounds, light, or electrical pulses.

Steven Birch, a scientist at Monash University in Melbourne, showed that entrainment of human body rhythms (as measured by an EEG) occurred during and after swims with free dolphins. The EEG of human subjects reduced in frequency and increased in power after swimming with free dolphins. So, in the sound field of the dolphins, humans will entrain to it. Dr. Birch believes that dolphin sounds trigger healthy, increased endorphin production and relaxation.

I asked Michael if listening to recorded dolphin sounds would also be helpful. He explained that some research indicates that recorded dolphin and whale sounds would, to some degree, create the same effect as live dolphin encounters.

Not only can humans benefit from receiving dolphin energy, but new research has also shown that we can create similar sonar waves ourselves, Michael explained. "When doing overtone chanting, it was found that ultrasound could be detected from the human forehead area above the nose (near the pineal gland or the 'third eye') at a range of about 30 feet in the air. So humans can *make* ultrasounds, also in the lower range of the dolphins."

Ultrasound exceeds 20,000 hertz. At one time, scientists believed that humans couldn't detect ultrasound, but a 1991 study at the University of Virginia showed that the saccule (a structure in the ear's vestibular system) could detect ultrasound up to 280,000 kilohertz. This is especially true underwater, since water conducts sound, according to work by researchers such as Martin Lenhardt of Virginia Commonwealth University, Dr. Patrick Flanagan, and Nassim Haramein. "Humans can perceive sounds in the dolphin range," Michael explained.

So, entrainment involves matching the energy signals you receive. In my soul-travel dream, I held two rulers, one plain-colored and one blue. I taught students to focus on the plain ruler and imagine that it exactly matched the blue ruler. The "blue ruler signals" I sent to the plain ruler made it entrain to match my thoughts. It turned blue because I saw it blue, and also because of the vibrations of an actual blue ruler nearby.

Entrainment is the ancient spiritual Law of Attraction wherein like attracts like. Every beginning metaphysical student knows that our thoughts attract and create our reality. Well, entrainment takes this one step beyond, into the world of creation through shape-shifting.

In Atlantis, the high-priest Hermes Trismegistus wrote the spiritual truths of alchemy on a tablet made of emerald. He wrote:

As above, so below

In other words, as we think (above), so we'll experience (below). As it is in Heaven (above), so it is upon Earth (below). This is also the basis for the spiritual Law of Cause and Effect, in which every effect is caused by a thought.

Hermes told me, *"All is thought. Affirmative prayers lift your thought to gratitude and love. These high vibrations attract more reasons to feel grateful and loving. It's possible to create and attract anything that your mind thinks about, believes in, and feels joy and gratitude toward. These thoughts and emotions of positive expectation set up a matching wavelength that creates or attracts what you're thinking about."*

His words reminded me of a study I'd included in my book *The Lightworker's Way,* which showed that when two people meditate next to each other, their brain waves synchronize. This synchronization then makes it easy for these individuals to give and receive telepathic messages to each other.

This effect may occur because of a cluster of frontal lobe brain cells called "mirror neurons." These cells fire not only when we're performing an action, but also when we see the same action performed by someone else. The mirror neurons don't distinguish whether we're the one snow skiing, for example, or whether we're watching a movie of someone else doing so. They fire identically in either case. Scientists believe that mirror neurons are one physiological basis of empathy, or the ability to feel someone else's feelings. They can also boost performance from visualizing success, or watching someone else's success. Mirror neurons synchronize you to whatever you're watching (one more reason to be discerning about the movies and other media we watch!).

This was entrainment of brain waves, and its applications and implications were seemingly endless! For instance, maybe we weren't absorbing other people's negative energies as commonly believed. Maybe we were entraining our own vibration to lower vibrations when we spent time with angry, dishonest, or depressed people! If this was true, then the reverse must also be possible: We

The Star of David and Mark of Vishnu.

could entrain others to a higher vibration by holding on to a positive mind-set no matter what was happening around us. This would be how Jesus, saints, avatars, and healers positively affected those in need.

Hermes illustrated the spiritual law of *As above, so below* with a hexagram, consisting of two intersecting triangles or pyramids, one pointing above, and one pointing below.

This symbol was later given to King David and passed to his son, King Solomon, who wore a ring with the hexagram and the sacred Hebrew name of God, *Yod He Vau He*, abbreviated out of respect with the letters YHVH. Solomon used this ring to invoke angels while building the temple that housed the Ark of the Covenant (the tablets Moses received from God). The symbols of Solomon's ring purified and lifted the energy of the temple, which protected it and its builders from lower energies.

The merman Matsya was the first incarnation of the Hindu deity Vishnu.

The hexagram is also known as the Mark of Vishnu, the primary Hindu deity who has incarnated as ten human avatars, including Krishna and Buddha. Vishnu first incarnated as Matsya, a merman who saved the Hindu sacred texts, *The Vedas*, during the flood.

So, words and symbols infused with ancient meaning purify and lift energy through the process of entrainment. Interestingly enough, ancient alchemists believed that the hexagram symbolized the elements of fire and water, with fire being above and water below.

Water exhibits the properties of entrainment. For example, homeopathy's foundation is water holding the energy of the symptom being treated. Scientific studies also show that water conducts vibrations, is affected and altered by human emotions, and stores information about nearby substances (even if that substance has never touched the water).

Studies on the electrical fields of Lourdes and other healing wells have been conducted by Dr. Enzo Ciccolo, a Milan biologist, the HeartMath research center in California, and other scientists. A study published by HeartMath says:

> Research has shown that water is a liquid crystal with a pliable lattice matrix that is capable of adopting many structural forms. The structure of water gives it an infinite capacity to store information within its matrix. A growing body of recent scientific evidence is now confirming traditional intuitive understandings of water's role as mediator between the energetic and material worlds and its function as an accumulator, transmitter and transducer of energy patterns and information. Much evidence points to water's ability to effectively memorize energy patterns with which it comes in contact and retain the energetic memory of vibrational frequencies for extended periods of time. Homeopathic medicine, for example, is based on water's capacity to store within its structural matrix the energetic imprint or vibrational signature of physical substances.
>
> A particularly striking example of water's "memory" of energetic information are the sources of water found throughout Europe at Marian sanctuaries, sites traditionally recognized as sacred, where apparitions of the Virgin Mary have been reported and numerous healings have taken place. These sites include Lourdes in France, Mediugorje in Croatia, Fatima in Portugal, and Montichiari and San Damiano in Italy. Recognized throughout the ages for their healing properties, the sources of water found at these sacred sites are believed to have recorded within them the frequencies of spiritual or higher dimensional energy associated with each of the sanctuaries.
>
> Scientific analyses have demonstrated that the Marian waters possess unique properties that are transferable to normal water through successive dilutions. Studies performed at the University of Milan showed that small quantities of the Marian waters added to normal tap water acted to modify the pH, conductivity and redox potential of the tap water. . . .

The crystallization of substances from solution is a phenomenon that has proven extremely sensitive to subtle energetic influences. We have shown that solutions of sodium chloride, sodium chloride and albumin, and cupric chloride to which a small quantity of the water of Mediugorje is added tend to crystallize in more finely divided, filamentary patterns than control solutions. These differences in crystallization patterns resemble those that have been observed in samples treated by healers' bioenergy and by magnetic fields.

In other words, water from healing wells associated with Mother Mary is structurally different from other water. Marian [from Mary] water stores the heartfelt prayers and the loving energy associated with Mother Mary and the angels. Studies show that this energy is transferable to ordinary water.

The water within our body's cells also entrains to prayers and healing energies (as well as to negative thoughts and harmful energies). I thought of the message I'd received from Sri Dhanvantari, the father of Ayurveda, who advised us to pray over *every* liquid we used, including eyedrops, shampoo, fruit juice, and the like. This would imbue those liquids with healing energy to support our overall health.

Of course, while others were writing and lecturing about water's ability to entrain thoughts, emotions, and other energies, one man was providing concrete evidence. Dr. Masaru Emoto, a Japanese scientist, had photographed crystals formed from water held next to various words and pictures. The most beautiful and beautifully shaped crystals came from water that was shown positive words such as *love* and *gratitude*.

I knew that I needed to meet Dr. Emoto. As I prayed over my drinking water one day while asking the goddesses and angels to arrange such a meeting, I felt a peaceful feeling in my gut that told me I'd get my wish. I let go of any thoughts about *how* this meeting would take place, and simply gave thanks to the goddesses and angels for their help.

❊ ❊ ❊ ❊ ❊ ❊

Chapter 22

Psychic Readings

In Brisbane Hall, as Leon Nacson, the director of Hay House Australia, walked me backstage, I strongly felt a presence. Leon apologized for taking me on a roundabout route to the stage, and I replied, "That's okay. This way, I got to meet the phantom of the opera!" I silently asked the phantom for permission to do our show there, and for his help that evening. A few minutes later I ran into Gordon Smith backstage and he told me, "There's a phantom of the opera here!"

The phantom did help me that night, or at least didn't interfere, but I did see a vision of my friend Judith Lukomski's face in the audience sitting in the balcony. I knew that Judith wasn't in Australia, but this was a gift from the spirit world to help me with my reading. So I went with it and asked the audience, "Is there a Judy or Judith sitting in the balcony?"

Two women raised their hands. Then I saw a television set and got the feeling that the Judith I was supposed to give a reading to worked in television. When I said this, one Judith's hand was still raised, and it turned out she did work in television, so I gave her a reading consisting of other messages I received from my visions and feelings.

Next, I heard the name Dahlia, and felt my body pulled to the right side of the audience. I'd never before heard that name, and several members of the audience said, "My name's Debbie!" or "My name's Donna!" A spirit voice repeated the name "Dahlia," so I insisted that she must be in the audience. Finally, a woman toward the back raised her hand and said she was Dahlia, and she was shocked that I'd called her name.

I told Dahlia of my vision of her in Egypt. "I've just been invited to go to Egypt!" she gasped. "I wasn't sure if I was supposed to go or not." I relayed the angels' message: She should definitely go.

The rest of the program went equally well, and then it was time to go to Melbourne for another workshop. Before the show, I visualized my readings being accurate and filled with blessings, and the audience being really pleased with everything. I visualized what I wanted instead of dwelling upon every psychic's fear of being blocked. This visualization helps a lot with my getting specific hits during my readings.

The Melbourne event was held at a Masonic facility, and an 18th-degree Mason gave me a tour of the Lodge and showed me the symbols and the giant G hanging in the ceiling for "God, the Great Architect and Geometrist."

As I'd prayed for and visualized, the readings at the Melbourne workshop were very accurate and filled with healing messages. That night I dreamed I was trying to call my mom to come get me, but the pay phones wouldn't work and I didn't have a cell phone. I'd been giving and nurturing so much to my audiences—and mostly traveling with Steven and the men from Hay House—that I needed to receive some Mother Love and female energy. I called my mom after I woke up, which helped a lot, and then after the Melbourne show, I rode back to the hotel with four women from the workshop staff. The girlfriend energy was very nurturing.

The next stop on our whirlwind tour was Brisbane. To refresh my energy, I went to the Brisbane City Botanic Gardens. I leaned against a banyan fig tree with lots of huge roots and trunks, and I heard it say, *"Move closer to my roots so the energy can be flushed away into the earth where it will be discharged."* As I lay on my back across the big root, I heard the tree tell me to release toxins into it, and also to absorb the loving energy that the tree was giving to me. I breathed in the tree's gift and exhaled out the energy of fatigue. I felt revitalized almost immediately.

The Angel Doctor

After Brisbane, we traveled to Perth on the other side of Australia. In that city, while giving audience readings, I looked up to the balcony and saw the cartoon character Dino the dinosaur from *The Flintstones* sitting in the audience. Even though my dragon power animal is named Dino, I knew in my gut and my mind that this vision meant that someone named Dino or Dina was sitting up there.

"Is there a Dino or a Dina up there?" I asked. A lady stood up and said she was Dina. Someone in the lower tiers of the hall also stood up and said *she* was Dina. But I insisted on the balcony, since that's where I'd seen Dino the dinosaur.

I could barely see Dina as she stood in the shadows of the crowded balcony. To give a reading in front of this audience of 2,000 people, I had to completely rely upon my inner visions, feelings, and thoughts. I'd learned to unhesitatingly report everything I saw in my mind's eye, even if it didn't make sense. Sometimes the messages came as gut feelings or a knowingness. Regardless of the form the Divine guidance took, I risked saying it into the microphone.

I saw an image of a heart superimposed over Dina, and I had the strong feeling that her heart had been recently broken. When I told her this, Dina began crying and said, "Yes, that's true."

Then I saw blood and cotton gauze, and I heard the word *hemorrhage.*

Dina replied, "That makes sense. I'm an emergency-room nurse, and I helped a hemorrhaging patient just today."

I told her that this was a double message about her work and her major heartbreak. I gave Dina some messages from the angelic realm concerning her love and work life. I was glad I'd learned to trust my inner sense, because during the entire reading, I couldn't see the woman at all. I could only hear her confirm the messages I relayed to her.

The next morning, the alarm clock woke me at 6 A.M. so that I could exercise before it was time to drive to a book-signing event. While doing sit-ups, I twisted my lower back, and it popped out of place. "Aarghh!" I muttered. The same thing had happened the prior year when I'd been in Perth.

At 10:30, Gordon Smith, Steven, and I were driven to a book signing at the Crystal Dolphin shop. Gordon and I entertained ourselves during the two-hour drive to Mandurah by doing impersonations and making up stories and doing silly voices. I think we drove our Hay House representative and the driver of the van crazy with our silliness, but that was how we passed the time.

Some may think it's glamorous to travel and give speeches, without realizing how much boredom and schlepping is involved. Our Australian tour, for instance, consisted of 12 people and multiple pieces of luggage and stage equipment. When we entered airports together, we received wary stares from overworked airline ticket agents.

That night at the Perth airport, a Qantas representative began hassling us about our carry-on luggage, saying that they were too heavy to bring on board. He wanted to weigh all of our carry-ons and make us check in anything over 12 pounds. I called upon the powerful Hindu deities Kali and Ganesh, and also Archangel Raphael, for help. Kali and Ganesh are wonderful for overcoming obstacles, and Raphael is the renowned angel of travelers. They'd helped me countless times while traveling in the past. At first I couldn't check in my crystal wand and my laptop computer, but then the Qantas representative backed down and let us through without any further hassle! Thank you, Kali, Ganesh, and Raphael!

On the airplane to Adelaide that night, we again felt bored with all the time it took to travel between locations. Gordon, Steven, the Hay House gang, and I played games by using the airplane headphones as pirate eye patches, Mickey Mouse ears, and *Star Trek The Next Generation* eyeglasses.

The next morning, I awoke in pain. My lower back was still out of place from the previous day's sit-ups, and I knew I needed help. When my back had gone out in Perth the year before, I'd finally gone to a chiropractor when I returned home. He'd popped my back into place in one visit, and I hadn't experienced further pain.

Steven and I prayed that we'd be able to find a good chiropractor in Adelaide. It was a scary thought to select a chiropractor in a strange city and country without a personal referral. "Please, God and angels," I prayed, "help me find someone who will pop my back into place, without drugs or x-rays, in one session."

We asked the hotel concierge to find a chiropractor who could see me that day. An hour later, the concierge said he was having trouble finding a chiropractor with any openings. Then he pointed to a phone-book listing and said, "There's one more doctor I haven't yet tried. I'll call his office next."

We went to breakfast in the hotel restaurant, and the concierge excitedly rushed over to tell us that the last chiropractor he'd called had just had a cancellation for 3:30 P.M. Since I was giving a seminar that evening in Adelaide, the timing was absolutely perfect.

As I dressed for the appointment, I worried that it was dangerous to pick a chiropractor randomly out of the phone book. Then a peaceful and powerfully reassuring feeling washed over me, and I *knew* with certainty that everything was in God's hands and fully taken care of. I knew that God had arranged for a wonderful chiropractor who would totally answer my prayers. As we rode in the taxi to the doctor's appointment, Steven said, "I sure hope this guy's good!" and I replied, "I know he will be." Then I told him about the reassurance I'd received from God.

As we walked through the door of the King William Road chiropractic office, Steven pointed to the sign and said, "Look at the doctor's name!" The sign read: Michael Angeli. Archangel Michael had protected me once again by sending me to his namesake.

Dr. Angeli looked like a cherubic incarnated angel, with large brown eyes and a shy smile. When I asked about his last name, he explained that it meant "angels" in Italian. Dr. Angeli gently popped my back into place in one visit, without using drugs or x-rays . . . just as I'd asked for in my prayers!

When I returned to the hotel, the angels told me that this experience was to help increase my level of trust. I began affirming, "I trust, I trust, I trust" to fully anchor this new realization. After all, I'd been learning on this tour to trust my inner wisdom enough to say everything I saw, felt, thought, and heard while giving public readings.

In a channeled flow of information, I was told to expand my affirmation to say, "I trust my inner supply and fountain of overflowing wisdom. I trust in *all* situations. Everything is in Divine order and going perfectly according to plan, even if I can't see, know, or understand that plan. I trust. I trust myself. I know that when we act with integrity and follow our Divine guidance, we have an easier time trusting ourselves."

The Healing Temple

I was now in Sydney, teaching a three-day Angel Intuitive course. I felt drained at the end of the tour of Tahiti and Australia and needed to be replenished. After a long and exhausting book signing, a woman came up to me and asked, "Can I give you a hug?" I heard the word *give* and imagined that she'd send me some energy, which I welcomed. So I exclaimed, "Sure!" She wrapped her arms tightly around me, and she burst into tears.

Oh no! I thought with panic as I felt her draining energy out of me. My level was already so low at that point, and this woman wasn't *giving* me a hug—she was taking one! I tried to push her off me, but her hands dug in.

Fortunately, a nurturing woman on the Angel Intuitive staff named Elizabeth Pearson recognized that I needed some mothering, since I'd been mothering so many others. I welcomed Elizabeth's pure, giving energy. She brought me warm herbal tea with lemon and honey to soothe my throat, which was tired after four weeks of daily talks and book signings. Elizabeth didn't ask for anything in return, which seemed unfortunately rare when I was on the road. What an Earth angel she was to me!

At the hotel that evening, I told Steven that I'd had recurring visions of a pyramid that housed priestesses who were sending me prayers and energy. I said, "I wish I could go into this temple in the pyramid and receive a large wave of healing energy."

He replied, "Well, why don't you?"

I then remembered that the mind doesn't know the difference between imagining and "reality," so I saw, felt, and imagined myself inside a pyramid with angelic high-priestesses sending me prayers and waves of colored energy, which washed over me with forceful currents, like a car wash. I felt my body shudder as it released psychic debris, cords, and toxins that I'd picked up on the road. I was now much more refreshed and ready to return home to California.

Courage

Once I was settled back in Laguna Beach, Lynnette and I decided to pursue advanced diving certificates. An Angel Therapist and dive instructor named Dave Ferruolo offered to give us private, advanced courses. The first one required us to swim downward to 90 feet. So Dave, Lynnette, and I took a ferry to the city of Avalon on Catalina Island on a chilly December morning. Although we wore full wet suits, plus neoprene hoods, vests, gloves, and booties, the 50-degree sea water felt shockingly cold. I looked at Lynnette's face, which had turned completely white from the frigid water.

I felt so cold that I considered skipping the dive. Then as we swam, I started to feel better. Wetsuits keep you toasty because they allow water in, which is warmed by body heat. The wetsuit then traps this water against the body, so you stay comfortable.

The beautiful Catalina kelp beds also distracted me from the water temperature. Just like an aquarium, the jungle vine–like kelp extended from the water surface to the ocean floor. Each vine was the diameter of a dinner plate, and they were spaced about three

Lynnette hands me a seashell talisman filled with love and blessings.

feet apart. Lynnette and I swam playfully through the sky-blue water in between the vines.

Dave pointed to his depth gauge and motioned for Lynnette and me to follow him. I gulped, realizing that it was time to go down to 90 feet. My deepest dive previously had been 45 feet. Would I be able to handle descending double that amount? I called upon Archangel Michael to protect me and give me courage.

Lynnette used hand motions to ask if I was okay. Using hand signals, too, I conveyed that I was frightened and wanted to return to shallower waters. Lynnette then dove to the floor of the ocean and scooped up a beautiful, empty seashell. She handed it to me and pressed it and my hand to my heart. I instantly felt safe, loved, and protected.

We then swam downward until there was nothing to see but blue water. The kelp and fish were above and behind us, near the shore. My depth gauge read 75 feet, and I made the mistake of looking up toward the water's surface. It was a long way up! I then felt my seashell talisman, which reminded me of the power of love. We kept swimming until Dave pointed to my depth gauge, which now read 95 feet! We'd done it!

We then turned around and returned to the more comfortable 40-foot level, amidst the sea kelp and orange garibaldi fish. After our dive, Lynnette explained that she'd felt guided to hand me the shell. During my brief moment of panic, I was able to entrain to the love with which the angels and Lynnette had imbued the shell, which had functioned as a talisman that gave me courage. I lovingly placed the shell on the bottom of the ocean, to disturb as little of the natural environment as possible.

My accomplishment of going 90 feet below water helped buoy my confidence in other areas as well. A few days following the dive, I ran into Andrea (the friend I mentioned earlier who always seemed to sap my energy). Normally, I would have feigned interest as she talked about her continual challenges.

This time, though, I told Andrea the truth. With calm and loving words, I explained why I'd been avoiding her. Even more surprisingly, she said that she understood! She admitted that *she* was sick of her constant struggles, and realized that she was creating and attracting them. She knew she needed counseling to work on why she always seemed to endure the same life patterns. As we hugged, I realized that this was my most genuine moment with her. I'd been true to myself and truthful to her. At that moment, I could swear I heard the *Rocky* theme song playing.

The next day, Steven and I learned that the escrow on our new home wasn't going well. April, our real estate agent, said the sellers discovered that they'd sold the house to us for far less than it was worth. They were trying to cancel the sale and our escrow, and it looked like they might be able to do so.

We were scheduled to move into the house in two weeks. We'd already fallen in love with it and were sure it was the home we were meant to live in. We'd affirmed, visualized, and stared at our dream-house collage, and imagined ourselves living in it. We couldn't lose the house now!

I called upon Kali, the powerful Hindu goddess who'd helped me so much since I'd begun working with her. You simply ask for her help and then get out of her way. Like a hurricane, Kali clears the path for you.

Well, Kali indeed cleared the way, and escrow on our dream home successfully closed. As April handed us the keys to our new house, I silently thanked the goddess for all she'd done.

The next week, my friends Karen and Evie told me that they were involved in a similar situation, where the sellers of their home were trying to cancel their escrow. I told Karen and Evie how Kali had secured ours for us. They immediately asked Kali to help them successfully close escrow. Although the situation looked dire, Karen and Evie got their home! Thank you, Kali!

* * * * * *

Chapter 23

WATER SOURCE

Steven and I drove to the La Jolla Hilton to meet with Dr. Masaru Emoto, the author of *The Hidden Messages in Water;* and his son, Hiro. Dr. Emoto was scheduled to give a talk at University of California at San Diego that evening, and he'd agreed to meet with us beforehand. I'd asked the goddesses and angels to help arrange an interview with Dr. Emoto, and my prayers had been answered.

On our way to the hotel, I telephoned to confirm our meeting, and the Hilton receptionist said that Dr. Emoto and his son hadn't yet checked in to their rooms. When we arrived, we were told the same thing. Steven and I decided to wait in the lobby. I asked Merlin, Raziel, and Michael to help bring about the interview.

About 20 minutes later, I spotted a young Japanese man whom I felt could be Hiro Emoto. I walked up to him and asked, "Are you Hiro?" He seemed relieved to find me, and said, "We just arrived at the hotel, and we're eating lunch in the restaurant. Do you mind waiting another 15 minutes?" I was happy the interview was still scheduled as originally planned, and said that I'd gladly wait.

Sure enough, 15 minutes later, Hiro appeared with his father, Dr. Emoto, who is one of the rare authors who actually looks like his publicity photographs. The four of us sat at a table in the lobby, and I gave them three of my oracle card decks, which had been translated into Japanese.

I asked Dr. Emoto why he thought all of the water crystals he's photographed have six points. He replied, "In geometry, the hexagon is the best shape to generate energy. A hexagon is two triangles intersecting, like the Star of David." There was the connection to the hexagon and water again!

I opened his book to the two photos of water crystals from Lourdes and also from water that was shown the word *angel*. The two photos looked similar. I asked why these water crystals weren't clear hexagons, and he pointed out that they were actually rings of hexagon crystals, which was even more powerful.

"Why do you think the Lourdes water photo and the angel water crystal look so similar?" I asked.

"When you talk about Lourdes, the first healing came from Mary, and she is connected with the angels," he replied. I recalled how strong the energy of angels was at the Lourdes grotto.

Water crystal that was shown the word *angel*.

Water crystal from Lourdes.

Dr. Emoto wrote in *The Hidden Messages in Water* that water is extraterrestrial and arrived on Earth in the form of lumps of ice from outer space: "If we go along with this theory of water being extraterrestrial, then perhaps we can better understand the many characteristics of water. Why does ice float? Why is water able to dissolve so much? Why is a towel able to soak up water, seemingly in defiance of the laws of gravity? From the standpoint that water is not of this world, these and other mysteries surrounding water may seem a little less difficult to understand."

I asked Dr. Emoto whether he believed that these ice comets contained DNA, and whether DNA itself had extraterrestrial origins.

He nodded and said, "Ice comets came from the universe as the origin of water. The origin of DNA is sent from the universe as a water crystal."

He then drew a picture of DNA, with its intertwining "snakes."

"These come from your parents," he said, pointing to the snakes. Then he drew two straight parallel lines like a straw inside of the intertwining DNA snakes. He pointed to this and said, "This information in the center is the water pole, which comes from the water comets." Dr. Emoto then added with a wink, "People who study the genes spend time studying where the water pole came from." He explained that health problems occur if the two snakes of the DNA strands don't coordinate with the inner water pole.

Dolphins and Atlantis

I then asked Dr. Emoto about dolphins, and Hiro turned to page 35 of his father's book. There was a picture of a beautiful hexagonal water crystal, and an explanation that this water had been shown a photograph of a dolphin.

Dr. Emoto pointed to a flowerlike shape in the center of the water crystal. I hadn't noticed any such shape in any of the other water crystals, so this in itself seemed unusual.

"It looks like a . . ." Dr. Emoto said something to his son in Japanese, and Hiro (who'd been translating our

© I.H.M General Institute. Image from: Messages from Water by Dr. Masaru Emoto, published by Hado Kyoiku Sha Co., Ltd. www.hado.net

Crystal from water that was shown a photograph of a dolphin.

interview into English) typed his father's words into a handheld language-converter machine. They both struggled to find English words to describe the center of the dolphin water crystal.

Finally, Hiro turned the language machine toward Steven and me, and we both read the English words simultaneously, "A pineal gland!" We looked at the photograph of the dolphin water crystal, and sure enough: its center did look amazingly like the gland that sits behind the third eye.

I pointed to my third eye to show Dr. Emoto that I understood his meaning. He nodded and said, "People came from the universe, and we have an antenna that connects us to the universe. This antenna is our pineal gland. Now, there are insensitive people who don't use their antennae, but the dolphins still use them. Dolphins are like brothers and sisters to us. They're still living in the sea freely, and that's one reason why they still use their antennae so accurately."

I asked Dr. Emoto if he thought that humans once lived in the sea, and he answered, "Of course! We used to live in the ocean."

"Do you believe in Atlantis?" I asked.

"I used to live in Atlantis," he replied.

"Me, too!" I practically shrieked, and Dr. Emoto beamed.

Dr. Emoto said, "I've been having dreams about Atlantis, showing how people are making the same mistake that we did there." He talked about water being a mirror of the human mind, and that we need to take care of both our thoughts and the water.

I asked Dr. Emoto if he thought that commercially bottled drinking water was healthful to drink, and he said yes, as long as we offer it a blessing of love and gratitude.

Then I asked Dr. Emoto if he considered love to be an active, male energy and gratitude to be a receptive, female energy, and he laughed. "I do believe that, but when I told my wife, she got mad at me," he said sheepishly.

Dr. Emoto explained, "Both love and gratitude together are very powerful, and the union of both vibrations creates the best and most beautiful water crystals. I believe that H_2O stands for two parts gratitude and one part love. That is the most powerful formula of all!"

"Water will be an even more critical factor in the future," he continued. "There are people who know that we can reduce pollution in the water through prayer. People's awareness of water is increasing. This time is different from past times, because more people know the importance of water."

Here I am with Dr. Masaru Emoto, author of *The Hidden Messages in Water.*

We then stood for photos, and Steven asked Dr. Emoto to smile. "I can't. I'm Japanese," he deadpanned.

As we drove home, I recalled Mother Mary's words at the healing waters of Lourdes, asking me to help the children. I also remembered Artemis asking me the same thing when I was in Sedona. I'd given many media interviews and seminars on the topic of the new Indigo, Crystal, and Rainbow Children . . . but there was something more I needed to do.

I entrained my bottle of drinking water with the intention of clearly knowing my Divine purpose in helping children. I asked Mother Mary, Artemis, and Archangel Metatron to let me know just how I could help.

A moment later, the answer came. With my background as an eating-disorders psychotherapist, I needed to ensure that school lunches were healthful and high quality. I shuddered, thinking about how many campuses served fast-food lunches around the world, and how this food impacted children's health, scholastic achievement, and moods.

I was shown a vision of how to help: I'd create a Website with free, downloadable charts illustrating the reasons why schools need healthier lunch programs. Parents and other interested adults could paste these charts on poster board and take them to school-board meetings. Several school districts had already banned soda and junk food based on parents' strong requests.

When we returned home, I hired a biologist to create the charts and launched the **schoollunchangels.org** Website.

❋ ▣ ❋

A large, pleasant-faced woman stood before me and asked me to sign her book. I looked up and said, "You're Greek, aren't you?" She nodded, and I gave her a big hug. Ever since visiting the Greek island of Santorini, a remaining fragment of Atlantis, I'd fallen in love with the warm-hearted Grecian people.

She asked me to give her a message as I signed her book. Immediately, the goddess Kali wrote through me onto her book:

I am a warrior goddess for peace,
and so are you.
Love, Kali

"Dolphins! Dolphins!" Steven nudged me awake out of my deep sleep, and the Greek woman and her book faded into dreamtime. He pointed to the window, where a large group of dolphins was swimming in front of our home. A big wave surged, and the dolphins surfed toward the shore. To our delight, one of these magical creatures jumped over the wave.

I was home . . . along with my family, the goddesses, the angels, and the dolphins.

❋ ❋ ❋ ❋ ❋ ❋

PART II

APPLYING THE KNOWLEDGE

Chapter 24

WORKING WITH GODDESSES AND ANGELS

Y ou can call upon goddesses and angels to increase your personal
power, confidence, and ability to heal and manifest. The
goddesses and angels are very happy to assist you with anything
that has a loving intention behind it.

Elements, with Corresponding Goddesses and Angels

Water	Air	Mother Creator Goddesses:
Aphrodite	Arianrhod	Aine
Asherah	Freyja	Arianrhod
Ixchel	Nut	Asherah
Morgan Le Fay		Hathor
Sedna	**Earth**	Ishtar
Yemanya	Bast	Ixchel
	Demeter	Mawu
Fire	Mawu	Sophia
Brigit	Persephone	Yemanya
Kali		
Pele	❊ ▣ ❊	
Sekhmet		❊❊❊❊❊❊
Vesta		

Which Goddesses and Angels to Call
Upon for Various Causes

Beauty
Aphrodite
Archangel Jophiel
Hina
Isis
Pele
Sedna
Xochiquetzal

Buying a Home
Abundantia
Archangel Ariel
Hecate
Hina
Kali
Lakshmi
Vesta

Children
Archangel Gabriel
Archangel Metatron
Artemis
Demeter
Hathor
Ixchel
(childbirth)
Mother Mary
Nut
Xochiquetzal

Clairvoyance
Archangel Raphael
Cerridwen
Freyja

Isis
Persephone
Quan Yin

Confidence
Archangel Michael
Artemis
Asherah
Astarte
Brigit
Isis
Kali
Pele

**Creativity
and Wisdom**
Archangel Gabriel
(for writing projects)
Archangel
Sandalphon
(for musical projects)
Archangel Zadkiel
Athena
Brigit
Cerridwen
Hecate
Hina
Isis
Ixchel
Kali
Sarasvati
(for music and the arts)
Sophia
Xochiquetzal
(for weaving)

**Fair and
Just Outcomes**
Archangel Michael
Archangel Raguel
Arianrhod
Astarte
Athena
Durga
Hathor
Ishtar
Maat
Rhiannon

**Fun, Play,
and Relaxation**
Bast
Freyja

**Health
and Healing**
Archangel Ariel
(for animals)
Archangel Gabriel
(for a child or
expectant mother)
Archangel Michael
Archangel Raphael
Asherah
Bast (for cats)
Brigit
Isis
Ixchel
Kali
Lakshmi
Persephone

Rhiannon
(from grief or for horses)
Tara
(White or Green)

**Household
Harmony**
Archangel Chamuel
Archangel Raguel
Athena
Hina
Isis
Ixchel
Sedna
Vesta

Increased Power
Archangel Michael
Artemis
Athena
Brigit
Kali

**Manifesting
and the Source-er
and Source-eress**
Archangel Ariel
Arianrhod
Cerridwen
Demeter
Fairies
Freyja
Hecate
Hina
Isis
IxChel
Kali
Morgan Le Fay

Sekhmet
Yemanya

Money Flow
Abundantia
Archangel Ariel
Hecate
Hina
Lakshmi
Sedna

**Physical
Strength**
Archangel Michael
Nut
Sekhmet
White Tara

Protection
Archangel Michael
Artemis
Astarte
Brigit
Cerridwen
Hathor
Hecate
Hina
Isis
Kali
Sekhmet
Xochiquetzal

Romantic Love
Aphrodite
Archangel Chamuel
Archangel Raguel
Arianrhod
Astarte

Freyja
Ishtar
Isis
Nut
Pele
Xochiquetzal

Traveling
Archangel Michael
Archangel Raphael
Hina
Isis
Kali

A Guide to Goddesses and Angels

Abundantia (pronounced *Ah-bun-DAHN-chee-ah*)

A Roman goddess of prosperity, money flow, and success, Abundantia helps to protect savings and investments; and can assist with major purchases such as a home, vehicle, or business venture. Roman legend says that Abundantia carried a cornucopia filled with coins and grain, which she'd leave as gifts in the households of sleeping people. You can ask Abundantia to help you with any issue related to money.

Aine (pronounced *AHN-yuh*)

An Irish sun and moon fertility goddess of environmentalism, protection, and love, Aine's name means "bright." She's a sorceress fairy queen who's said to give grass its sweet smell. Aine also protects women, animals, and the environment. She's celebrated with a torch-bearing procession on Midsummer's Eve. You can call upon Aine for psychic and physical protection, source-ery, and banishment, and to connect with the fairies.

Aphrodite (pronounced *Af-ro-DY-tee*)

A Grecian goddess of Venus, love, and beauty, Aphrodite's name means "foam born," as she was conceived after her father, Uranus (the sky god), impregnated the sea womb. Although the beautiful Aphrodite was married to Hephaestus, she had numerous affairs with Greek gods. This led to her reputation as a goddess of love, romance, sexuality, beauty, and passion. You can call upon Aphrodite to assist you with any aspect of romance.

Archangel Ariel (pronounced *AHR-ee-el*)

Her name means "lioness of God," and she's an archangel (meaning that she's a powerful overseer of guardian angels and humankind). Ariel helps wild animals, especially waterfowl and seabirds. She's also involved with manifesting supply for humans and animals. Call upon Ariel for healing animals (especially those in the wild), environmental concerns, and manifesting.

Archangel Chamuel (pronounced *SHAM-you-el*)

His name means "God sees," and this archangel is wonderful at seeing everything. Call upon Chamuel to help you find lost objects, and listen carefully for the accurate guidance that he'll give you in the form of a thought, feeling, or vision as to the object's whereabouts. Chamuel also engenders peacefulness. Ask Archangel Chamuel to help you with personal inner peace, peace within relationships or situations, and world peace.

Archangel Gabriel (pronounced *GAB-ree-el*)

Her name means "messenger of God," and she's the archangel made famous by the Gospel of Luke for telling Mary and Elizabeth of the forthcoming births of Jesus and John the Baptist, respectively. Gabriel continues to help expectant mothers through all phases of motherhood. Call upon Gabriel to help you with child adoption, conception, pregnancy, and birth. As the messenger angel, she also assists journalists, writers, speakers, and teachers.

Archangel Jophiel (pronounced *JO-fee-el*)

This archangel's name means "beauty of God," and she'll beautify every area of your life. She's a "feng shui" angel, meaning that she'll compel you to clear your space by donating unneeded items, straightening your living or work areas, and filling your space with items imbued with high energy (like crystals, plants, and flowers). Jophiel can help with any aspect of aesthetics, such as guiding your wardrobe, hair, or makeup. Call upon Jophiel if your thoughts become negative, and she'll instantly beautify your mind with positive ones.

Archangel Metatron (pronounced *MET-uh-tron*)

The ascended prophet Enoch, who worked with Hermes in Atlantis, Metatron is one of two mortal men who became archangels, the other being Archangel Sandalphon (who was the prophet Elijah). Metatron is named a chief angel in the Kabbalah's Tree of Life, and his main role in modern times is to assist the new psychic and sensitive children (the Indigo and Crystal Children). Along with Mother Mary, he guides the life path and purpose of Indigo Children, and helps their parents and teachers. If you'd like to help the Indigo Children, ask Metatron for a Divine assignment. You can also call upon him for assistance with children's behavioral issues.

Archangel Michael

His name means "he who looks like God," and Archangel Michael is one of the most powerful members of the spirit world. This tall, handsome angel carries a sword of light to release us from fearful attachments. He's a fiery archangel who guides our life's purpose with loving but to-the-point advice on how to work on our purpose without delay. He's also Divinely wise about fixing electronic and mechanical items. Call upon Michael to increase your courage; and to provide protection for you, your loved ones, and your vehicles and property.

Archangel Raguel (pronounced *RAG-you-el* or *RAG-well*)

His name means "friend of God," and he is brilliant at healing relationships. Call upon Raguel if you've had a misunderstanding with a friend, co-worker, romantic partner, or family member. He helps everyone to soften their heart and to forgive and forget.

Archangel Raphael (pronounced *RAFF-ee-el*)

His name means "God heals" or "he who heals," and this archangel is the supreme healer of the angelic realm. Raphael also retrieves and finds lost pets. Call upon him to heal any condition in yourself or another. Although he can't impose healing upon someone else without their consent, Raphael's presence brings comfort and peace wherever he's called. You can also ask Raphael to guide your healing career, including helping you to select a modality, training program, and location for your healing practice; and also to bring you wonderful clients.

Archangel Raziel (pronounced *RAH-zee-el*)

This archangel's name means "secrets of God," and he knows all the esoteric secrets of the universe. It's believed that he gave Adam an instructional guide about Earth life. Call upon Raziel to understand esoteric dreams, to learn sacred geometry and other ancient secrets, and to heal from past lives. Raziel can help you release fears of being psychic, which stem from being killed in previous incarnations.

Arianrhod (pronounced *Ahr-eye-UN-rod*)

An ancient Welsh moon and fertility goddess, Arianhrod is the daughter of Dana (Goddess Mother of the Irish Tuatha Dé Danann). Arianrhod's name means "silver wheel," a nod to her moon-sorceress connection. She claimed to be a virgin, but a test by the wizard Math revealed that she was pregnant. Soon after, Arianrhod gave birth to twin boys, one of whom was a merman. Arianhrod is considered a magical weaver, and she's often invoked to "weave spells."

Artemis (pronounced *AR-tem-is*)

The Greek moon goddess and protectress of women, children, and animals, her twin brother is Apollo and their father is Zeus. Artemis is often confused with the Roman goddess Diana, although they're separate beings with differing characteristics. Artemis carries a bow and arrow, and she spends most of her time in the woods with wild animals. Call upon Artemis to protect you, your children, or animals; you can also ask her to help during childbirth. In addition, Artemis helps women develop their inner strength and courage, especially with regard to helping other women, children, animals, or the environment.

Asherah (pronounced *AW-sher-ah* or *ASH-ay-raw*)

A Canaanite Mother Creator goddess who's sometimes referred to as "Asherah of the Sea," because she's said to have conceived her 70 deity offspring in the ocean, Asherah is frequently mentioned in sacred Hebrew texts as the wife of God (El or Yaweh). Canaanites carried wooden totems dedicated to Asherah, and she was invoked for healings. Call upon Asherah for nurturing, healing, and courage to stand by your spiritual beliefs.

Astarte (pronounced *Ah-STAR-tay* or *Ah-STAR-tee*)

One of Asherah's offspring, Astarte is a Phoenician goddess of war and love, and her name means "she of the womb." She's associated with the star Venus, and temples were built in her honor. Historians equate Astarte to goddesses in Egypt (Isis) and Babylon (Ishtar), although she has a distinct personality and energy. Ancient myths speak of Astarte's penchant for making love to various gods, and she was invoked during battles for wisdom and protection. You can call upon Astarte to resolve arguments with a romantic partner, to protect you, and for sacred sexuality.

Athena (pronounced *Uh-THEE-nuh*)

Also known as Pallas Athena, she's the Greek goddess of wisdom. Athena wears a helmet to symbolize her role in wisely resolving conflicts and wars. She's a goddess of weaving, crafts, and art. Call upon Athena for wisdom, help with arts and crafts, and protection.

Bast (pronounced *Bast,* with an "a" as in "at")

The Egyptian feline goddess who's portrayed as a lioness or cat, Bast oversees dancing, music, and fun. And like a cat, she's highly independent. Call upon Bast when you need to lighten up, to become more independent, or to help a pet cat.

Brigit (pronounced *Breed, BREE-ged, BRIDG-It,* or *BRI-dee*)

An ancient Celtic sun goddess of healing, fertility, and protection, Brigit was later initiated as a beloved saint of Ireland. February 1 is her Celtic holy day, called Imbolc, celebrating the return of the spring sunshine after the dark winter. A flame in her honor burns in Kildare, Ireland, commemorating Brigit's fiery persona, and her name, which means "bright arrow" or "powerful one." Brigit is regarded as a triple goddess who incorporates the Maiden, Mother, and Matriarch aspects of goddesshood; for this reason, you can call upon her to help with virtually anything. She's especially helpful in areas of motivation, healing, and arts and crafts.

Cerridwen (ponounced CARE-uh-dwen)

Cerridwen is a Welsh fertility goddess of inspiration, creativity, knowledge, poetry, and growing grains. Legend says that she created a magical elixir for her son, who was so physically unattractive that she wanted to help him compensate with brilliant intelligence. The elixir would make her son the most clever man in the world. A servent helping to brew the elixir tasted it and instantly became omniscient. In honor of this legend, ancient Celtic rituals heat cauldrons filled with water and flowers on a fire to consecrate them with Cerridwen's magic. You can enhance your creativity by placing a pot of water (or a cauldron if you have one) on your stove and asking Cerridwen to infuse it with her blessings.

Demeter (pronounced *Dem-EE-ter*)

A Greek earth, fertility, and mother goddess, Demeter is the daughter of Hecate and the mother of Persephone. This family represents the triple goddess's influence on changing seasons. Legend says that Persephone was kidnapped by Hades and taken to the underworld. During this time, Demeter was so depressed that she neglected the earth's vegetation, so no crops grew. Zeus finally helped her to find Persephone in the underworld. While Demeter was there, Persephone ate pomegranate seeds and was allowed to return to the upper world to help her mother care for the earth. Yet, because she had eaten of the underworld fruit, Persephone had to return three months yearly—the time of winter when crops hibernate. You can call upon Demeter to help grow literal or figurative crops in your life, and to celebrate springtime when winter thaws and Persephone is reunited with her mother.

Freyja (pronounced *FRAY-uh*)

Freyja is a beautiful, eternally young Nordic air goddess of love, sexuality, and romance. The day Friday was named for this fun-loving goddess. Freyja travels in a chariot that large cats pull along the rainbow pathway between Heaven and Earth. Nordic myths say that both men and giants lusted after her, and she loved to read erotic poetry. Freyja practiced the Nordic magic called *seid,* which involves women sitting in a circle and singing invocations to deities in a séance. This allows the women to see into the future. Call upon Freyja when you need to relax and have fun, for romance and sexuality, and for source-ery, clairvoyance, or prescience.

Hathor (pronounced *HATH-or*)

An Egyptian Creator goddess and mother of the sun god, Ra, Hathor is usually depicted as a mother cow. This symbolizes the milk she fed to Ra and baby pharaohs to instill them with Divine energy. At birth, one of seven aspects of Hathor was assigned to a baby in a divination tool known as the Seven Hathors. Ancient Egyptians viewed her as the primary love and sexuality goddess, and ceremonies in her honor involved a lot of music and dancing.

She is also regarded as an underworld and a sky goddess. Hathor can help with new projects, and all aspects of mothering.

Hecate (pronounced *HEH-caw-tee*)

A Greek moon goddess of the night who brings protection, abundance, and success, Hecate is also the mother of Demeter and grandmother of Persephone. She represents the matriarchal phase of the triple goddess and the waning moon, and her symbols represent her triple-goddess aspect. For example, she's usually portrayed as an older woman standing at the crossroads of three paths, walking three dogs. Sometimes, she's painted with three heads. She's a wise and powerful source-eress, and you can call upon her for manifesting and protection.

Hina (pronounced *HEE-nah*)

A Polynesian Creator moon goddess who is so beautiful that no one can look directly at her, Hina gave humankind tapa cloth from banyan trees for clothing and income. Hina is also the wife of the god Kane, and she provides protection for warriors and travelers and helps artists and craftspeople. Call upon her to watch over you while traveling, to make your inner light shine brighter, and for help with artistic careers.

Ishtar (pronounced *ISH-tar*)

A Babylonian goddess representing the moon and Venus, Ishtar is a triple goddess, meaning that she embodies the Maiden, Mother, and Matriarch aspects of womanhood. Legends tell of Ishtar's descent into the underworld, and she's a powerful helper in exploring a woman's shadow sides. Call upon Ishtar for any female issue, including sexuality, motherhood, and protection.

Isis (pronounced *EYE-sis*)

The Egyptian daughter of Nut and Geb, sister of her husband Osiris, and mother of Horas, Isis raised Osiris from the dead after their brother Seth killed him. In their joyful reunion, they conceived Horas. Isis convinced the sun god, Ra, to reveal his secret name to her, thereby giving her magical powers. Isis was one of the first traveling spiritual teachers, giving information to Egyptian women about weaving, beauty, herbal remedies, motherhood, and relationships. She's depicted with wings, and a sun disk or throne upon her head. Call upon Isis for help with any issue related to motherhood or womanhood, for source-ery, and herbology.

Ixchel (pronounced *EE-shell*)

The Mayan moon, water, and Mother goddess who watches over childbirth and provides healing, Ixchel is a Creator goddess who gave birth to all the gods (along with her husband the sun god). She moves through the sky with the moon, away from her husband in a show of independence. As a water goddess, Ixchel controls the rain flow and is called "Lady Rainbow" because her light shines through water droplets like prisms. Call upon Ixchel for help with healing or childbirth.

Kali (pronounced *CAHL-ee*)

The often-misunderstood, powerful Hindu goddess of endings and beginnings, Kali ushers in life and escorts away death as the goddess of cycles and renewals. Kali is one of the more powerful goddesses, and she has a forceful way of ensuring that her goals are met. This forcefulness frightens some people, particularly those who don't want to face endings as a natural cycle of life or those who are intimidated by powerful women. Many stories discuss Kali's ability to protect through destruction, but she's loving and fair even when we don't understand the mysteries of beginnings and endings. Call upon Kali when you have an urgent need for powerful help; however, don't tell her how to effect your desired outcome. Just ask for her help, and then get out of her way while she goes to work on your behalf with Divine power and wisdom.

Lakshmi (pronounced *LOCK-shmee*)

A Hindu and Buddhist goddess whose name means "goal" or "aim," Lakshmi is a beautiful goddess of prosperity and wife of the sun god Vishnu. She also works closely with Ganesh, the beloved Hindu elephant-headed deity who overcomes obstacles for people. Lakshmi is considered both an Earth fertility goddess and a water goddess who sprang from a lotus blossom in the ocean. Call upon her to help you manifest abundance, to stop worrying about money, and to attain joy and happiness.

Mawu (pronounced *MAH-woo*)

An African moon and sky Creator goddess, Mawu created the world and its human inhabitants. However, she became distressed at the behavior of humans, so she retreated to the sky. In her place, she sent her son, Lisa, to manage the earth's daily affairs. She intervenes in issues concerning the environment and helps humans to live in harmony with nature. Call upon Mawu for a Divine assignment to help preserve nature.

Morgan Le Fay

A Celtic goddess of the sea and of fairies (*Mor* means "ocean," and *Le Fay* means "of the fairies"). Morgan Le Fay is a queen of Avalon, the former island that now forms Glastonbury, England. She's sometimes confused with the Celtic moon and underworld goddesses called The Morrigan. Morgan, who learned source-ery from Merlin and was half-sister to King Arthur, can help you connect with water elementals, as well as the magic of Avalon and Merlin.

Mother Mary

Mary is the modern-day Mother goddess who's also known as the "queen of the angels." As with many goddess traditions, she was a virgin when she gave birth to her son, Jesus. Mary's apparitions are reported around the world, and these visitations are associated with miraculous healings and vital messages. Mary helps anyone involved with children, including parents, teachers, and healers, so call upon her to help with any aspect of parenthood, or to give you a Divine assignment so you can assist children.

Nut (pronounced *Noot*)

Nut is the Egyptian sky goddess who gave birth to Isis, Osiris, and Seth, whom her brother, the earth god Geb, fathered. She is sometimes represented as a cow, and other times as a woman arching over the earth (she assumed this position to reach her beloved earth brother when Ra the sun god forbade their incestuous relationship). Call upon Nut for issues related to your love life or motherhood.

Pele (pronounced *PAY-lay*)

Pele is the Hawaiian fire and volcano goddess who's sometimes credited with creating the earth's big flood. Many stories talk about her jealous battles with her ocean goddess sister, including fighting over Pele's husband and island territory. Call upon Pele to recognize and live by your true passion, and to ignite the flame of enjoyment for your relationships and career.

Persephone (pronounced *Per-SEF-uh-nee*)

The Greek daughter of Demeter and granddaughter of Hecate, Persephone represents the Maiden aspect of the goddess. When Persephone is upon the earth, she makes flowers and trees bloom, but when she's in the underworld, trees and plants are barren. Call upon Persephone for help with gardening, any issue related to a young girl, or to help with new beginnings.

Quan Yin (pronounced *Kwahn Yin*)

The Buddhist Maiden goddess of compassion, Quan Yin means "she who hears and answers all prayers." Quan Yin is sometimes spelled Kwan Yin or Cannon. She's a bodhisattva, meaning that she's eligible to ascend into Buddhahood. However, Quan Yin has elected to stay near the earth, helping people until everyone is enlightened. Call upon Quan Yin when you need help forgiving yourself or another, for issues related to women and children, and to increase your sensitivity and clairvoyance.

Rhiannon (pronounced *REE-aw-non*)

A Welsh moon goddess who takes souls from the earth to the spirit world while riding a white mare and accompanied by three magical birds whose song awakens the dead, Rhiannon was falsely accused of her son's murder. Call upon her with issues related to transition and death, as well as help with false accusations. (She also helps horses.)

Sedna (pronounced: *SED-nuh*)

An Eskimo and Inuit ocean goddess who provides food and sustenance, Sedna was a Maiden who lost her fingertips in a boating accident. Her fingertips subsequently became the seals, dolphins, and other ocean mammals. Call upon Sedna to help supply you and your family with groceries and other household needs. She'll also help you with boating, surfing, swimming, and diving, provided that you're respectful of the ocean's inhabitants.

Sekhmet (pronounced *SEK-met*)

An Egyptian warrior goddess whose name means "powerful," Sekhmet is associated with lions or with a lion head as a sign of her strength. Sekhmet is the daughter of the sun god Ra, and she breathes fire to protect those she watches over. Call upon Sekhmet when you need protection, courage, or inner strength.

Sophia (pronounced *So-FEE-uh*)

The Gnostic and Judaic goddess of wisdom, Sophia is an ancient Creator Mother goddess and counterpart to Ishtar and Astarte. She's portrayed in the Bible as Jehovah's companion. In some traditions, Sophia created the *Elohim* (deities, gods, or goddesses) and the angels. Call upon Sophia for wisdom, clear thinking, and practical reasoning. She also assists with the arts and crafts.

Tara

A Hindu and Buddhist goddess whose name means "star," Tara is shown growing from a lotus flower to symbolize her birth from the stars. Her many aspects are represented by colors: When her face and body are green, she's the fast-paced rescuer who comes to our aid in crises.; when she's white, she helps us experience longer, more peaceful lives. Call upon Green Tara to help you overcome any obstacle, and White Tara to help calm your mind and body.

Vesta

Vesta is the Roman fire Mother goddess of hearth and home. In ancient Rome, a flame in her honor was tended by the Vestal Virgins. The Romans believed that Vesta resided with each household's fireplace, ensuring warmth and comfort within the home. Call upon Vesta to warm up your relationships, home, career, or life in general.

Xochiquetzal (pronounced *So-she-KETZ-el*)

An Aztec and Toltec eternally young and beautiful Maiden goddess also known as "Flower Feather," Xochiquetzal is an earth and fire element fertility goddess who brings about love and passion. She's also considered a protective Mother goddess and patroness of unmarried women, new mothers, and weavers. Call upon her for help with any aspect of romance and motherhood.

Yemanya (pronounced *Ye-MAHN-jay*)

An African and Brazilian water Mother goddess who's celebrated with white flowers and prayer requests thrown upon the ocean each New Year's Day, Yemanya is considered the Mother Creator of the ocean and freshwater sources. Her body pours forth the streaming waters of the rivers, and she brings prosperity and supply in Divine order. Call upon her to answer your prayers, especially concerning women's issues and getting your needs met.

※ ※ ※ ※ ※ ※

BIBLIOGRAPHY

Ann, M. & Imel, D. M., *Goddesses in World Mythology.* New York: Oxford University Press, 1993.

Bardon, F., *Initiation into Hermetics.* Salt Lake City, Utah: Merkur Publishing, Inc., 2001.

Batmanghelidj, F., *Water for Health, for Healing, for Life.* New York: Warner Books, Inc., 2003.

————, *Your Body's Many Cries for Water.* Vienna, Virginia: Global Health Solutions, Inc., 1997.

Bernstein, H., *Ark of the Covenant, Holy Grail.* Marina del Rey, California: DeVorss & Company, 1998.

Black, J. & Green, A., *Gods, Demons and Symbols of Ancient Mesopotamia.* Austin, University of Texas Press, 2003.

Buchman, D. D., *The Complete Book of Water Healing.* New York: Contemporary Books, 2002.

Calleman, C. J., *The Mayan Calendar and the Transformation of Consciousness.* Rochester, Vermont: Bear & Company, 2004.

Clark, P.J., *The Sorcerer's Handbook.* New York: Sterling Publishing Co., Inc., 2001.

Climo, S., *A Treasury of Mermaids.* New York: HarperCollins Publishers, 1997.

Coulter, C. R. & Turner, P. *Encyclopedia of Ancient Deities.* Jefferson, North Carolina: McFarland & Company, Inc., 1997.

Editors, Time-Life Books. *Dragons: The Enchanted World.* Chicago: Time-Life Books, 1984.

Ellis, R., *Aquagensis.* New York: Penguin Books, 2001.

Emoto, M., *The Hidden Messages in Water.* Hillsboro, Oregon: Beyond Words Publishing, Inc., 2004.

Epstein, P., *Oriental Mystics & Magicians.* New York: Doubleday & Company, Inc., 1975.

French, C., *The Celtic Goddess.* Edinburgh: Floris Books, 2001.

Gadon, E. W., *The Once & Future Goddess.* San Francisco: HarperSanFrancisco, 1989.

Hardy, A., *Darwin and the Spirit of Man.* London: Collins, 1984.

Hart, G., *A Dictionary of Egyptian Gods and Goddesses.* London: Routledge, 1986.

Hawley, J. S. & Wulff, D. M., *Dévi: Goddesses of India.* Los Angeles: University of California Press, 1996.

Hoult, J., *Dragons: Their History & Symbolism.* Glastonbury, Somerset, 1990.

Howard, M., *Angels & Goddesses.* Chieveley, Berks (UK): Capall Bann Publishing, 1994.

Jennings, S., *Goddesses.* Carlsbad, California: Hay House, Inc., 2004.

Jones, K., *The Ancient British Goddess.* Glastonbury, Somerset (UK): Ariadne Publications, 2001.

Keenan, S., *Gods, Goddesses, and Monsters.* New York: Scholastic, Inc., 2000.

Kindred, G., *The Earth's Cycle of Celebration.* Derbyshire, UK: Glennie Kindred Publisher, 2002.

Knight, C. & Lomas, R., *Uriel's Machine.* Gloucester, Massachusetts: Fair Winds Press, 2001.

Lao, M., *Sirens: Symbols of Seduction.* Rochester, Vermont: Park Street Press, 1998.

Lindow, J., *Norse Mythology.* New York: Oxford University Press, 2001.

Lundy, M., *Sacred Geometry.* Powys: Wales: Wooden Books, Ltd., 1998.

McCoy, E., *A Witch's Guide to Faery Folk.* St. Paul, Minnesota: Llewellyn Publications, 1999.

———, *Celtic Myth & Magick.* St. Paul, Minnesota: Llewellyn Publications, 2002.

Meyerowitz, S., *Water: The Ultimate Cure.* Summertown, Tennessee: Book Publishing Company, 2001.

Miller, M. & Taube, K. *The Gods and Symbols of Ancient Mexico and the Maya.* London: Thames & Hudson Ltd.

Monaghan, P., *The New Book of Goddesses & Heroines.* St. Paul, Minnesota: Llewellyn Publications, 2000.

Montgomery, D., *Aquatic Man and African Eve.* Suffolk, England, 2005.

Morgan, E., *The Aquatic Ape.* New York: Stein and Day, 1982.

———, *The Descent of Woman.* London: Souvenir Press, Ltd., 2001.

———, *The Scars of Evolution.* Oxford: Oxford University Press, 1994.

Muten, B., *Goddesses: A World of Myth and Magic.* Cambridge, Massachusetts: Barefoot Books, 2003.

Nigg, J., *The Book of Dragons & Other Mythical Beasts.* Hauppauge, New York: Barron's Educational Series, Inc., 2002.

———, *Wonder Beasts.* Englewood, CO: Libraries Unlimited, Inc., 1995.

Passes, D., *Dragons: Truth, Myth, and Legend.* New York: Golden Books, 1993.

Patai, R., *The Hebrew Goddess.* Detroit: Wayne State University Press, 1990.

Pennick, N. & Field, H., *The Goddess Year.* Chieveley, Berks (UK): Capall Bann Publishing, 1996.

Penwyche, G., *The World of Fairies.* New York: Sterling Publishing Co., Inc., 2001.

Pogâcnik, M., *Nature Spirits & Elemental Beings.* Forres, Scotland: Findhorn Press, 1995.

Rivera, A. *The Mysteries of Chichén Itzá.* Universal Image Enterprise, Inc., 1995.

Rose, C., *Giants, Monsters & Dragons.* New York: W.W. Norton & Company, 2000.

———, *Spirits, Fairies, Leprechauns, and Goblins.* New York: W.W. Norton & Company, 1998.

Ryrie, C., *The Healing Energies of Water.* Boston: Journey Editions, 1999.

Schauberger, V., *The Water Wizard.* Dublin: Gill & Macmillan, Ltd. (No Date Given).

Schiff, M., *The Memory of Water.* London: Thorsons, 1994.

Shipley, J. T., *Dictionary of Word Origins* (Second Edition). New York: The Philosophical Library, 1945.

Sjöö, M. & Mor, B., *The Great Cosmic Mother.* New York: HarperCollins Publishers, 1991.

Spretnak, C., *Lost Goddesses of Early Greece.* Boston: Beacon Press, 1992.

Stewart, R. J., *Celtic Gods, Celtic Goddesses.* London: Cassell & Co., 1990.

Stone, M., *When God Was a Woman.* Orlando, Florida: Harcourt Brace & Company, 1976.

Telesco, P., *365 Goddesses.* San Francisco: HarperSanFrancisco, 1998.

Temple, R., *The Sirius Mystery.* Rochester, Vermont: Destiny Books, 1998.

Tomasino, D., *New Technology Provides Scientific Evidence of Water's Capacity to Store and Amplify Weak Electromagnetic and Subtle Energy Fields.* Boulder Creek, California: Institute of HeartMath, 1997.

Trobe, K., *Invoke the Goddess.* St. Paul, Minnesota: Llewellyn Publications, 2000.

Turner, P. & Coulter, C. R., *Dictionary of Ancient Deities.* New York: Oxford University Press, 2000.

Virtue, D., *Archangels & Ascended Masters.* Carlsbad, California: Hay House, Inc., 2003.

———, *Goddess Guidance Oracle Cards* (guidebook). Carlsbad, California: Hay House, Inc., 2004.

———, and Lukomski, J., *Crystal Therapy.* Carlsbad, California: Hay House, Inc., 2005.

Wilkinson, R.H., *The Complete Gods and Goddesses of Ancient Egypt.* London: Thames & Hudson, 2003.

Wilson, C., *From Atlantis to the Sphinx.* New York: Fromm International Publishing Corp., 1999.

Zhang, S. N. & H. Y., *A Time of Golden Dragons.* Toronto: Tundra Books, 2000.

✻✻✻✻✻✻

Resources

Amma information
- *Website:* **www.amma.org**

Ayurvedic Healing
- **Shannon Kennedy,** clinical Ayurvedic specialist and body worker, Medical Rejuvenation Center, Newport Beach, California. (949) 644-4566

Crystal Bed Healing
- **Chris Marmes**, Laguna Beach, California.
  E-mail: AtlanteanHealing@aol.com

- **Kelly Willis,** Mountain Home, Idaho. (208) 599-2018

Crystal Therapy
- **Judith Lukomski**, Dana Point, California.
  Website: **www.crystalfriends.com**

Dolphin Channeling and Readings
- **Lisa Weiss**, Laguna Hills, California. *Website:* **www.dolphinscalling.com**
  E-mail: DolphinsCallingU@aol.com

Dolphin Research
- **Michael Hyson, Ph.D.** *Website:* **www.planetpuna.com**

❀❀❀❀❀❀

ABOUT THE AUTHOR

Doreen Virtue PhD is a clairvoyant doctor of psychology who works with the angelic, elemental and ascended master realms in her writing and workshops. Dr Virtue has lectured extensively around the world on the topics that she discusses in her books, and she has appeared on many television programmes such as Oprah and CNN. She is the author of many bestselling books, including Messages from Your Angels and Healing with the Angels.

Doreen has appeared on *Oprah,* CNN, *The View,* and other television and radio programs. For more information on Doreen and the workshops she presents throughout the world, to subscribe to Doreen's free e-mail angel-messages newsletter, to visit her message boards, or to submit your angel healing stories, please visit **www.AngelTherapy.com**.

You can listen to Doreen's live weekly radio show, and call her for a reading, by visiting **www.hayhouseradio.com**™.

✳ ✳ ✳ ✳ ✳ ✳

Hay House Titles of Related Interest

BORN KNOWING: *A Medium's Journey*
by John Holland, with Cindy Pearlman

THE DISAPPEARANCE OF THE UNIVERSE:
Straight Talk about Illusions, Past Lives, Religion, Sex, Politics, and the Miracles of Forgiveness, by Gary R. Renard

THE GOD CODE: *The Secret of Our Past, the Promise of Our Future,*
by Gregg Braden

MENDING THE PAST AND HEALING THE FUTURE WITH SOUL RETRIEVAL,
by Alberto Villoldo, Ph.D.

PRACTICAL PRAYING: *Using the Rosary to Enhance Your Life,*
by John Edward (published by Princess Books, distributed by Hay House)

POWER ANIMALS: *How to Connect with Your Animal Spirit Guides*
(a book-with-CD), by Steven D. Farmer, Ph.D.

SACRED CEREMONY: *How to Create Ceremonies for Healing, Transitions, and Celebrations,* by Steven D. Farmer, Ph.D.

SECRETS & MYSTERIES OF THE WORLD,
by Sylvia Browne

SPIRIT MESSENGER: *The Remarkable Story of a Seventh Son of a Seventh Son,* by Gordon Smith

THE UNBELIEVABLE TRUTH
by Gordon Smith

TRUST YOUR VIBES: *Secret Tools for Six-Sensory Living,*
by Sonia Choquette

❋ ▣ ❋

Available at all good bookshops, or may be ordered by calling
Hay House Publishers direct on 020 8962 1230.

ALSO AVAILABLE BY DOREEN VIRTUE, PhD

BOOKS

Price £9.99

Price £9.99

Price £9.99

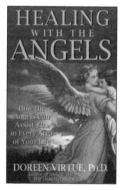

Price £9.99

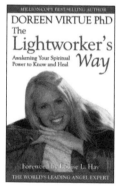

Price £9.99

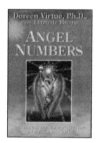

Price £4.99

Available at all good bookshops or by calling
Hay House Publishers direct on 020 8962 1230
www.hayhouse.co.uk

ALSO AVAILABLE BY DOREEN VIRTUE, PhD

CARD PACKS

Price £11.99

£11.99

£11.99

Price £11.99

£11.99

Price £11.99

Available at all good bookshops or by calling
Hay House Publishers direct on 020 8962 1230
www.hayhouse.co.uk

ALSO AVAILABLE BY DOREEN VIRTUE, PhD

CDs

Price £14.99

Price £7.99

Price £14.99

Price £7.99

Price £7.99

Price £15.99

Available at all good bookshops or by calling
Hay House Publishers direct on 020 8962 1230
www.hayhouse.co.uk

HAY HOUSE PUBLISHERS

Your Essential Life Companions

For the most up-to-date
information on the
latest releases, author
appearances and a host
of special offers, visit

www.hayhouse.co.uk

Tune into **www.hayhouseradio.com**
to hear inspiring live radio shows daily!

Unit 62, Canalot Studios, 222 Kensal Road, London W10 5BN
Tel: 020 8962 1230 E-mail: info@hayhouse.co.uk

❋ NOTES ❋

❋ Notes ❋

❧ Notes ❧

❋ NOTES ❋

We hope you enjoyed this Hay House book.
If you would like to receive a free catalogue featuring additional
Hay House books and products, or if you would like information
about the Hay Foundation, please contact:

Hay House UK Ltd

Unit 62, Canalot Studios • 222 Kensal Rd • London W10 5BN
Tel: (44) 20 8962 1230; Fax: (44) 20 8962 1239
www.hayhouse.co.uk

✱✱✱

Published and distributed in the United States of America by:

Hay House, Inc. • PO Box 5100 • Carlsbad, CA 92018-5100
Tel: (1) 760 431 7695 or (800) 654 5126;
Fax: (1) 760 431 6948 or (800) 650 5115
www.hayhouse.com

Published and distributed in Australia by:

Hay House Australia Ltd • 18/36 Ralph St • Alexandria NSW 2015
Tel: (61) 2 9669 4299 • Fax: (61) 2 9669 4144
www.hayhouse.com.au

Published and distributed in the Republic of South Africa by:

Hay House SA (Pty) Ltd • PO Box 990 • Witkoppen 2068
Tel/Fax: (27) 11 706 6612 • orders@psdprom.co.za

Distributed in Canada by:

Raincoast • 9050 Shaughnessy St • Vancouver, BC V6P 6E5
Tel: (1) 604 323 7100 • Fax: (1) 604 323 2600

✱✱✱

Sign up via the Hay House UK website to receive the Hay House
online newsletter and stay informed about what's going on with
your favourite authors. You'll receive bimonthly announcements
about discounts and offers, special events, product highlights,
free excerpts, giveaways, and more!
www.hayhouse.co.uk